HAS THE AMERICAN MEDIA MISJUDGED CHINA?

Thirty five years after China's opening to the world, some of the key
assumptions that have guided coverage are being tested
by the presidency of Xi Jinping

Edited by William J. Holstein for The Overseas Press Club of America
Based on a reunion of current and former China-based correspondents

CONTENTS

INTRODUCTION

In many respects, American media coverage of China today is excellent, extending far beyond the imagination or capabilities of previous generations of correspondents. One reason is that news organizations have made major commitments to covering China. The Chinese Foreign Ministry accredited 682 foreign journalists in 2013 and Hong Kong, which was reunited with the mainland in 1997, remains a major journalistic outpost as well. These correspondents were able to root out and cover the scandal surrounding leading Communist Party official Bo Xilai, his wife and his security chief in a way that previous generations of correspondents would not have been able to do. *The New York Times* and Bloomberg News also penetrated into the secrets of the Chinese leadership's network of personal financial connections far better than any previous generation could have done.

But a reunion of about 70 current and former China Hands—the largest such gathering devoted to the period since China re-opened to the world in 1979—examined some of the media's underlying assumptions about China over the sweep of the decades. (See APPENDIX A for a list of attendees.) Those assumptions, by their very definition, shape coverage, and assumptions have misguided the media in its coverage of China at different points in history. Media coverage of the civil war between the Nationalists and Communists did not fully convey the corruption and incompetence of the Nationalists partly because editors at home such as *Time*'s Henry Luce wanted positive coverage of Generalissimo Chiang Kai-Shek. Years later, some in the Western media believed China was experimenting with its version of a socialist paradise during the 1966-1976 Cultural Revolution and did not realize that 10 million people were being killed because of their ideological views and class backgrounds.

Nor did the media fully understand the enormity of China's economic emergence in 1979. The media, believing in the inevitability of political change, also could not imagine that Deng Xiaoping would dispatch tanks and other heavy weaponry to smash the demonstrations in Tiananmen Square in June of 1989. After he did, the media then believed that such a massacre would certainly curtail China's economic aspirations. But instead, the country resumed impressive double-digit economic growth starting soon thereafter. Likewise, the media was profoundly skeptical that the Chinese could build an entirely new commercial and industrial city across the Huangpu River from the Bund in Shanghai, but the Chinese did successfully build the vast Pudong district. The outside world, shaped by the media's coverage, has consistently misjudged China.

The assumptions that have been in play in recent coverage include these: As hundreds of millions of Chinese in a broad middle class move into cities and make economic gains, they will seek greater political clout for themselves. The Communist Party, as part of a process nicknamed "peaceful evolution," will be obliged to cede some power to a more civil society at the local level. No one has believed the Party would share power as part of a two-party political system at the national level, but some stirrings of pluralism at the local level have been widely predicted. Another belief has been that, as the Chinese engage more robustly with the world in terms of trade, investment, education and tourism, such intercourse would introduce liberal Western influences and soften the grip of the Party.

In this hopeful view, the Chinese would accept the existing world order established by the United States following World War II and be a "responsible stakeholder" in it. It would continue to allow foreign companies to operate with relative freedom in the vast Chinese market. Other more recent pieces of this positive view were that the Internet would allow many Chinese to give voice to their opinions, challenging the Party's political monopoly, and that the Chinese would continue to respect the theory of "one country, two systems" in Hong Kong. One might call this general line of expectation the soft China theory.

But the reunion, held on Sept. 12, 2014 in New York, concluded that many of these assumptions are proving unrealistic under the presidency of Xi Jinping, who has been in office for two years and will be in office for eight more. Although China is charging into an embrace with the world in terms of trade, investment, education and tourism, Xi is not allowing the blossoming of a civil society at home. In fact, legal reforms are seeking to eliminate the decision-making power of local courts. Lawyers who represent dissidents are being arrested, not just the dissidents. Minorities such as the Uighurs and Tibetans are being dealt with harshly.

Elsewhere, the government has cracked down on a vibrant social media scene. The government also is taking a tough line against the Western media, hacking their websites, denying visas to correspondents and shutting down their Chinese-language websites, as described by the latest policy paper of the Foreign Correspondents Club of China. (A summary is in APPENDIX B. The OPC protest statement is APPENDIX C.)

In short, China is expanding internationally, but its domestic situation is headed in the opposite direction, as some panelists noted. Rather than following in the footsteps of Japan, South

Korea and Taiwan, which undertook democracy under U.S. military and diplomatic pressure, China seems to be following the model of Singapore, which has allowed no political opposition to the ruling Lee family.

The expectation that China's emergence on the world stage would be benign, meanwhile, is being tested by its declaration of an Air Defense Identification Zone in contested waters of the East China Sea and constant military pressure on Japan, Philippines and Vietnam over disputed islands. Reflecting its buildup of its blue-water navy, Beijing does not appear to be willing to accept the world order that the United States and others established after World War II, but instead is intent on challenging it over time. Economically, foreign companies are being targeted by new anti-monopoly powers and the suspicion is unavoidable that Chinese authorities are taking these steps to bolster Chinese national champions.

All these trends suggest that the China that's emerging is a very different China than what many in the media expected. When Xi spoke of restoring the "China dream" of strength and stability, it appears now that there is a tough edge to the dream, as seen from a Western perspective. The police crackdown on protesting students in Hong Kong came after the Sept. 12 China Hands reunion and that confrontation has been now been defused. But the official Chinese tone toward the demonstrators was initially so severe that many observers were concerned that it would either force the Hong Kong police to use greater violence or would call out the People's Liberation Army units stationed in Hong Kong, risking another Tiananmen-style massacre.

The new tone in the Chinese leadership, and in the relationship between the United States and China, was perhaps best captured by Orville Schell, who was first a reporter in China in 1974 and is now director of the U.S.-China Center at the Asia Society in New York. "The Chinese are much more resistant to whatever kind of pressure is brought to bear" on them for change in their economy or society, Schell told the reunion.

"Just a few days ago I was with a friend who is an American official whose judgment I deeply respect," he continued. "We were talking about how China is in a transition. He said, 'Economically yes, politically no. You can forget about your civil society. You can forget about your democratization. You can forget about human rights. You can forget about all these things. They are not going to happen. They are not on the agenda. If you want to have good relations, don't go there.' I thought that was a stark wake-up call."

Schell concluded: "This is a very new and increasingly vexing dynamic we are going to have to deal with. This raises a really stark question if you believe, as I do, that somehow or another, we have to cooperate with China in terms of climate change, pandemics and nuclear proliferation. Are the democratic countries of the West willing to accept China for what it is? Until that happens, and I'm not advocating it, we are going to find China continuing to be in this very complicated relationship with us where they are resisting all the time and we're not going to be able to get to solve any of these really big problems that trump everything else. We're in a tipping point moment."

The reunion was held at Club Quarters in New York. It included a series of four panel discussions on how the American media is covering China. These workshops touched on coverage of China's economy; the contradictions of a China that has improved living standards for millions even if it has not allowed creation of a civil society; China's treatment of the Western press on the mainland and in Hong Kong; and lastly, the tug-of-war between those Chinese and Westerners who are seeking to use social media and the Internet to break through the so-called Great Firewall of censorship that Chinese authorities have erected. The correspondents were joined by a handful of non-journalistic experts and the proceedings were videotaped. (Many segments are available at www.opcofamerica.org.)

The correspondents ranged in age from their 20s to their 90s. The oldest correspondents, Roy Rowan and Seymour Topping, covered the Chinese Civil War from 1947 to 1949. Another generation of correspondents covered China from outside the country during the 1949-1979 period when it was closed to the outside media, relying on radio broadcasts, newspaper reports and occasional visits. One participant, Jaime FlorCruz, has been stationed in Beijing for 40 years with the exception of one year spent outside the Middle Kingdom. Wide coverage from inside China resumed when Western news organizations were able to re-establish bureaus in late 1978 and at the beginning of 1979, some 35 years ago.

The reunion was arranged by an organizing committee of China Hands who were mostly members of the Overseas Press Club of America: Marcus Brauchli, Dorinda Elliott and Adi Ignatius, Pete Engardio, Jocelyn Ford, Peter Goodman, William J. Holstein, Susan Jakes, Roy Rowan, Seymour and Audrey Topping, and Minky Worden and Gordon Crovitz.

The Foreign Correspondents Club of China (FCCC) and the Asia Society's ChinaFile acted as co-sponsors. The FCCC was represented by Jocelyn Ford and ChinaFile by Susan Jakes. It was felt that bringing together journalists of multiple generations from multiple organizations and multiple cities (New York, Washington, and Beijing, primarily) would produce a higher quality of understanding about China coverage over the long term. I served as chair of the organizing committee and this account is my interpretation of what was said that day. Any errors or misinterpretations are mine and mine alone.

I would like to thank the board of the Overseas Press Club for sponsoring the event and also Executive Director Patricia Kranz for helping to organize it. Thanks also to Lesley Topping for providing videography services and to Chad Bouchard for help in covering the event and in creating the cover for this book.

- William J. Holstein

PANEL 1

American Media Coverage of China's Economic Emergence

Most Americans know that China's economy is likely to exceed America's in size in coming years, but what does that mean? Does China's emergence pose a direct threat or are its internal challenges so serious that it won't be able to make the leap to advanced industrialized status? How good of a job is the American media doing in addressing these issues?

MODERATOR

William J. Holstein, who was based in Hong Kong and Beijing from 1979 to 1982 for United Press International, is currently a business journalist and author most recently of "The Next American Economy: Blueprint For a Real Recovery." He is a former president of the OPC and a member of its board.

PANELISTS

John Bussey, assistant managing editor and executive business editor of *The Wall Street Journal,* is the author of a weekly column on global business trends. He has been based in both Tokyo and Hong Kong.

Pete Engardio covered China's economic and business scene as a Hong Kong-based correspondent for *BusinessWeek* from 1990 to 1996 and then as a New York-based writer and editor until 2009. He received multiple OPC awards for his work and is co-author of *"Asia's Boom, Bust, and Beyond."* He is now a senior writer at The Boston Consulting Group.

Orville Schell, director of the Center on U.S.-China Relations at the Asia Society, has covered China since 1964 for *The New Yorker*, *Atlantic*, *New York Review of Books*, and other top publications. His latest book on China, *"Wealth and Power: China's Long March to the Twenty-First Century,"* was published this summer.

Holstein: This is a panel on whither China's economy and how the America media covers it. We all know that the Chinese have amassed nearly $4 trillion in foreign exchange reserves and that their economy is going to be bigger than ours at some point. The International Monetary Fund says it already has happened in terms of purchasing power. The prospect of China being larger than our own economy is seen with great dread if you read the newspapers and listen to supposedly expert opinions. If you think back about our coverage of China's economy, it has veered from wildly optimistic to hugely pessimistic. We don't seem to have been able to achieve a consistent point of view or line of analysis. Perhaps we can make some progress on that today.

Holstein to Orville Schell: You arrived in 1974 in the middle of the Cultural Revolution. How poor were the Chinese at that point?

Schell: The suggestion that things would go the way they did, with China emerging so strongly, couldn't have been imagined at that time. This was a country that tore itself down and had to reinvent itself completely. I don't think there are too many cases of that happening in world history. Not the French Revolution, or even the Russian Revolution. They were not as thorough and as systematic as China's experience. It has reinvented itself economically speaking into a form of authoritarian capitalism. But there are other pieces of the other whole proposition which seem firmly in place ever since the Mao years. There is a

12

discontinuity between the economic changes and whatever may happen politically and culturally and in terms of values. There are huge gaps in this whole proposition which haven't been fully realized. That makes China incredibly unstable and makes it very difficult for anybody to predict the future because at the same time there are all these equal and opposite things happening at the same time. It's trying to find who it's going to be in its new guise. Economically speaking, they have come up with something they are starting to actually believe in, which is an alternate model. But we don't hear so much anymore the discussion about reform being a double–barreled proposition with both a political element and an economic element.

Parenthetically, I was just there with former President Jimmy Carter. They treated him extremely poorly. It was a humiliation for him, having gone there to celebrate 35 years of diplomatic relations after his incredible moment with Deng Xiaoping in 1979. The message of how they treated Carter was that, here is a country still very much up for grabs in terms of its identity and trying to cling to the part that has changed in significant ways, namely the economy. The wager going forward is this: can a country, a society, which once did have deep and profound traditional culture, a values system and a social structure, can it survive only reinventing one part of the overall proposition, namely the economy? I'm dubious about it. But I have to say I've been dubious for 25 years. And yet it has cohered.

Holstein: I arrived in Hong Kong in January 1979 after Jimmy Carter and Deng Xiaoping normalized relations. My organization, United Press International, decided that the journalistic stars in our company—the A team, if you will—should open the bureau in Beijing. They would send out the B team kids from New York to Hong Kong to supplement the regional news desk. I was part of that. But Bob Crabbe and Aline Mosby, in our Beijing bureau, found themselves asking, "Where's the story? What's happening

13

in this country?" The northern part of the country remained absolutely the way it had been before normalization.

But part of my job was to cover the Canton Trade Fair in the southern city of Guangzhou and to cover the special economic zones in that province of Guangdong, such as Shenzhen. The big question everyone in the outside world was asking was, can the Chinese really overcome socialist class struggle and massive bloodletting to turn their attention to economic reform? I didn't speak a word of Chinese. But I began writing how about it looked to me like the Chinese were throwing off the class-struggle version of socialism and were really more focused on getting material things. This was at an era when a foreigner could attract crowds of people who would just look at you. They looked at your watches, your sunglasses, your pen, your clothes, everything. Those were the things they wanted. I also started to write about the special economic zones. I saw how the Chinese were organizing themselves. They were applying a massive amount of labor but it was focused on one thing—on getting wealthy. It wasn't focused on class struggle. That was the key insight I had as a 28-year-old writing about the country from Hong Kong. Nobody in the world knew whether the Chinese could emerge economically or not. Now flash forward 35 years, and they are the world's second largest economy.

Q. Turning to John Bussey, what years did you spend in Hong Kong and what were your first impressions? Did you sense how the story would turn out?

A. I first lived in Hong Kong in 1982 and 1983 and my first visit to China was in 1983. I share Orville's sense of wonder about all this. In the past 20 years of the *Journal's* coverage, we have reported all these reservations about China's prospects. Each time, China has proved us wrong—but at some point we'll get it right. (Laughter.)

My first trip to China was five years after economic reforms had been announced. Not a lot had happened. The bureaucratic machinery was still galvanizing around this modernization idea. Things were pretty much the same as they had been for several decades. In Shanghai, you looked out from the Bund across the Huangpu River and there was no Pudong district across the river. It was just warehouses and some farms. Just 20 years later, you have an entire city there. I remember going back in 2005 to Shanghai and I was crossing the street. There was a young man parked in the middle of the street, 20 feet from the curb. All the more way for him to showcase his possession which was this fabulous Hummer he had bought. It was a cherry-red chariot and had these big fog lamps on top and big grill work in the front. The whole point was to be so apparent that people couldn't help but stop and marvel at his possession. I'm not a Mandarin speaker but I approached him and asked, "My, what a beautiful Hummer." He couldn't speak any English but he pointed at the windshield and said in English, "Night vision." Then he pointed at the hood and said, "Turbocharge." (Laughter.)

I'm thinking this is, in a way, emblematic of what happened to the country in those intervening 20 years. It was ramping up an economic system whose sustainability we had questioned all along. It was pushing out exports out the door. It had a social compact in which the government said, "We are going to improve your lives economically. You leave the politics to us." That compact has worked for 30 years. The question now is whether or not the structural problems that we and everyone else have been predicting will become problematic for China. There's not enough of a private sector. Half of the non-agrarian economy is run by state-owned enterprises (SOEs). There is an immense patronage system run through the SOEs that the Communist Party is going to have a hell of a time dismantling. Add in the problems of corruption and pollution. There's also a huge debt mountain. Will

15

the social compact be violated to the point that there is some kind of social instability?

But again, I remember going to Beijing in the late 1990s. It was one of the periods when the press, including the *Journal*, was negative about China. There was an inflation problem, among other issues. We talked to a one of the deputy economic ministers. We said, "Look, you have all these problems."

He rolled his eyes and shook his head and said, "We're not Alan Greenspan. We can't turn the dial a quarter of a turn and adjust monetary rates as finely as he can. But we have our ways." What he was talking about was administrative measures he could take. He could call up the banks in a province and stay "Stop lending." And the bank presidents would stop lending for fear that their kids wouldn't get into college or whatever leverage point top officials might have. But at a certain point, the economy becomes too big for that to be effective. The question is whether now, we're at that point in China.

Holstein: Pete Engardio started out covering South Korea in 1979 before making his way to the Hong Kong and China story in 1990. We worked together at *Business Week*. I was his editor in New York and used to tell him that we needed to add more perspective and meaning to his stories. I kept saying that we needed to step back and ask ourselves what all this means. At one point, Pete said to me, "Bill, if I step back any more I'm going to fall out the window. (Laughter.)
Here's Pete Engardio.

Engardio: I came to covering China with a frame of reference, which was South Korea. That country was regarded as a model for development, going from extreme poverty to wealth. We have been trying to get our arms

16

around the story of China for all these years. We've struggled to understand this economy and what its model is exactly.

I'd like to take you down memory lane a bit and show you how the business media's perception of China has evolved. I'll tell the story through *BusinessWeek* cover stories. (Some images included.) I wish to thank *Bloomberg/BusinessWeek* for generously sharing as many digital images of old covers as they could locate and for also allowing me to borrow old bound volumes of the magazine so that I could scan other covers.

We started out in the 1980s with covers like this one, "Capitalism in China," published in 1985. Chinese consumers were starting to look more and more like us. The images we saw were of Coca-Cola bottles on the Great Wall, Deng Xiaoping with his cowboy hat. China was one of the best feel-good stories of the 1980s. Hundreds of millions of people were rising out of poverty, which was an amazing accomplishment. It looked like China was going to become a market economy but was also going to open up politically, the first big Communist power to do so.

Then Tiananmen Square happened in 1989 and shattered that kind of illusion. *BusinessWeek's* cover story was called "China: The Great Leap Backward." The crackdown created obvious disappointment about where China was headed and doubts about whether it could continue to go forward with reforms.

After Tiananmen, we sank into a year or two of tea-leaf reading. Are Li Peng and Chen Yun going to roll back reforms? Is Deng Xiaoping going to prevail? Is Zhao Ziyang going to come back? By around 1992, it was clear China was back on track. Deng had made his famous trip to southern China, where he put his support behind continued economic reforms. Vice Premier Zhu Rongqi came along. (Engardio shows a cover story with Zhu's image and the language: "China: Building The New Economy.") The coverage became positive again. There were many intelligent, English-speaking people in charge we could interview. They were driving really hard.

Westerners have long been accused of projecting our own image onto China, wanting the Chinese to look like us and become like us. This was one of my covers, which was optimistic. (He holds up a cover entitled, "China's New Elite," published in June 1995, featuring a handsome Chinese executive for an American company in China.) In the mid-1990s, a young post-Cultural Revolution generation was rising up into leadership positions. This was a very optimistic cover that meant to say, "Look, don't demonize this country. There are a lot of really good people."

By around 1996, the perception in the media started changing. We had the Taiwan Straits crisis and the Wen Ho Lee affair, when it was feared that Chinese scientists were stealing all our secrets. Then came the Donor Gate scandal during the Clinton Administration. There was a feeding frenzy. Was China trying to buy out our political system? Cover stories reflected the zeitgeist of how China was seen in the United States. This cover story

("China," published in May 1996) asked the questions, "Is China really opening? Is it really going to become a fair trade partner? Is it going to be a responsible world partner?" There was a lot of introspection. By 1997, there were serious doubts about whether Zhu Rongqi's reforms were really going to take hold. (Cover story: "China: Can It Really Reform Its Economy?" published in September 1997.)

Holstein: "Reform" is such a loaded term whenever you apply it to China.

Engardio: Yet we held out hope. Covers like "China's Web Masters" (published in August 1999) reflected the increasing sophistication of China, illustrated by the growth of the Internet and the presence of brilliant technology talent. The next year, we published the cover "China's New Entrepreneurs" (published in May 2010), which explained how China was acquiring a private sector. The story was that China was evolving out of socialism. The state's role was declining. It was something of another feel good era. China had backed off

on Taiwan. There were some points of contention, to be sure. But as China geared up to join the World Trade Organization (WTO), our optimism reached a new point with the cover, "China's Opening: The promise and peril of the WTO deal" (published in November 1999). The cover depicts China and the U.S. shaking hands.

Then the dark side of China starts creeping in again. We start focusing on the underbelly. We became obsessed with China's counterfeiting. (Holds up a cover reading, "China's Pirates," published in June 2000.) China was ruthlessly copying all our products, which became a recurring theme. Then we had a cover story entitled simply "China: Should We Engage?" It asked whether we should engage with China or not. Is China our big partner in the world or is it a threat? We didn't know. China had two faces.

But on the other hand, China was still progressing. This cover entitled, "High Tech China" (published in November 2002), said the country was making great technological strides. But it was kind of a back-handed compliment. If you read the deck language, we asked, "Is it a threat to Silicon Valley?" That's what we were concerned about. Is China the next Japan times five or six? It has 10 times more engineers than us. Should we be worrying about this? We weren't seeing it as a great contribution to the world. In 2004, we came out with the "The China Price" (published in December 2004). By this time, China is  in the WTO. All of our manufacturing work seemed like it was heading to China. It seemed like we could not compete. No matter what was manufactured, it seemed like China could make it 40 percent cheaper—telecom networking equipment, furniture, bedroom sets, everything. The bedroom sets were made with wood from the United States and shipped back and they were still 40 percent cheaper. We were worried China was wiping out our jobs and there was nothing we could do about it.

Then we entered the "shock and awe" era of China coverage. All of a sudden, China is a rising superpower, whether we like it or not, good or bad. This cover was about Greater China, about the power of the combined economy of China, Taiwan, and Hong Kong. (Published in December 2002). This cover was a big double issue that we ran on China and India. (China and India: What You Need to Know," published in August 2005). It was basically about why the economies of China and India will dominate the world. Get used to it.

But then we returned to the seamy side pretty quickly, because we were getting kind of tired of the rise of China. This cover entitled, "Secrets, Lies, and Sweatshops," was published in November 2006 (below). We tried to take a more sophisticated look at the topic, asking whether it was the Wal-Marts or Targets, with their pricing and costs strategies, that were really causing the problem. We then started worrying about the environmental disaster that is developing in China, food problems, the corruption. (Holds up cover entitled: "Can China be Fixed?,"

published in July 2007). We asked, "Is China really a superpower? Or is it in reality just a really dysfunctional place?"

By now, the tone is getting really negative. I am going to show you some covers of *BloombergBusinessWeek*, and again I wish to thank *BloombergBusinessWeek* for sharing them. This cover was about China acquiring property in Australia. (Holds up cover entitled, "Property of China," published in September 2010.) Points to image of the Sydney Opera House with a Chinese flag painted on it.) Basically, China is buying up the world. They are buying up our precious assets, similar to when the Japanese bought up major New York office buildings.

Here's another. It reads, "Hey China. Stop Stealing our Stuff!" (published in March 2012.) Forget about nuance now. Here is another. "Lies, Lies, Lies," (published in May 2012). This is about the Bo Xilai affair and how the culture of greed, violence, and deceit has permeated the system. Here is one more, "Yes, The Chinese Army Is Spying on You," (published in February 2013). So that settles that.

In sum, we are all still struggling to understand China. I don't think we have made much progress on that. But I do think it is clear that China has settled into a political and economic system. The reform era in China has lasted longer than the pure Communist model. It was 30 years from the end of the revolution in 1949 to the opening of 1979 and they've been reforming for 35 years since then. They have settled into a model. Barring really drastic changes of the political system, we'll continue to be puzzled by it.

Holstein: We know that a huge number of jobs have moved to China. Our companies are there in wholesale fashion. We know the Chinese are competing with us for raw materials around the world. But so far they have not launched an assault on what we might regard as our strategic industries—semiconductors, airplanes, or cars. The Chinese, for example, have not yet been able to export cars yet to the United States. So the question is whether the Chinese emergence will pose a direct threat to American economic interests and how we define ourselves as a high-value added economy. Do you feel that the Chinese model will allow them to steamroller our position?

Schell: The day before yesterday I was in Washington at a dinner sponsored by the U.S. semiconductor association and I was guiding a discussion. There were 35 CEOs of semiconductor companies in the room. Their topic was, do we have a future in China? Increasingly, I hear companies speaking quite darkly about their prospects in China whereas previously businesses were the heart and soul of the booster class advocating better relations with China. That's quite an interesting change.

The other big change we're right on the precipice of, and it's actually begun, is China's foreign direct investment into the United States. In the semiconductor world, I heard the first purchase has been made of an American semiconductor company.

Holstein: Are the American companies worried that they are not going to have a market in China or do they see competition emerging from Chinese players?

Schell: They are wary that they are going to be squeezed out of China. The Chinese are investing $50 to $100 billion, so they say, to create state-owned competitors, like they did in solar energy. The Chinese are willing to invest exactly what many of the more sober senators and congress people in this country think we should be investing. But when the Chinese do it, of course, it's called unfair trade practices. There are a lot of huge changes on the horizon. I wonder whether American and European investment in China will continue to expand as rapidly as it has in the past. But it's clear that we are going to see a lot of Chinese money coming out.

Holstein: Orville, we often talk about how the Chinese model consists of state-owned enterprises controlled by the Party, which strikes many of us as not being very competitive in the world. Are they capable of making the leap to the most advanced industries or is this model going to hold them back?

Schell: This is the big question, isn't it, whether China is sufficiently high on the periodic table of innovation. My view is if you look at it as a spectrum, China can get pretty high up on the spectrum. They may not engage in primary innovation. But they can do a lot of tinkering across that scale to get value added. They may not have a lot of people doing theoretical physics and what not. But I wouldn't discount the ability of the Chinese to squeeze enough out of the innovation equation to have substantial benefit for themselves. The West may continue at the very top end to have a monopoly. But who knows? That could change too.

Holstein: John Bussey, what is your opinion?

Bussey: On the technology curve, there's no question that China will be at the very top along with us and other parts of Europe. It's just a question of time. They have a new generation of engineers in the country. They have the ability to learn from the West by going to the West and ripping off technology and applying it to their own country. Anybody who doubts whether China has the innovative acumen need only look back at history to see that they do.

Holstein: Here is the nation that created gunpowder and paper. They changed the world. But so far, in this iteration, they have not done that.

Bussey: Well, you have more than 1.3 billion people with big aspirations. They will be right at the top of the curve. They are already much further up the curve than anyone would have thought.

Turning to this issue of American business attitudes, during China's ascension to the WTO, the business community in the West were the advocates of China. They were doing the door knocks all around Capitol Hill. Now it's completely changed. The latest American Chamber and U.S.-China Business Council surveys all show a majority of businesses say they are getting hammered by the new anti-monopoly laws in China. By latest non-tariff barrier that China is using to screw the Westerners. It follows on from indigenous innovation, which our former colleague Jim McGregor wrote about this fabulously for the Chamber of Commerce, which used very extensively to hammer foreigners in select industries where China wants to build its own national champions. It's going to do so. The anti-monopoly law is being used to fix some pricing issues but it is being used primarily to hold foreign companies at bay. Even though the survey results are as bad as they are, more than 90 percent of these companies are still reporting profits out of China. There is an inevitability to Western involvement in China regardless of how badly Western companies are treated and increasingly Western diplomats like Jimmy Carter are treated.

I was at a meeting of the National Committee on U.S.-Chinese relations last night and we were talking about energy in China. China is now the biggest energy consumer in the world, having bypassed the United States. This trajectory in energy consumption, in innovation, all of this is going to build these national champions. And they are going to compete incredibly effectively against the United States, not just because of state subsidies, but because they've learned how to compete internationally.

Engardio: I have been a skeptic about China's ability to compete at the high end for many years because of my Korea experience. How many people here today have a Haier (a Chinese brand) refrigerator in their homes? (Only a few hands are raised.) China has had big consumer appliance companies for 20 years now. It took Korea's Samsung and Lucky Goldstar about 20 years to start manufacturing and exporting to the United States and becoming some of the biggest companies in the world. You don't see a Chinese company anywhere close. It's something they ought to be strong in. A lot of the production has gone to China for the rest of the world. They have all these engineers. But this pattern goes through their whole portfolio of industries. You don't see any Chinese company except for Huawei and ZTE getting close to the cutting edge.

Holstein: Lenovo as well. They bought IBM's personal computer division and have been able to use the acquisition to build a truly multinational technology company.

Engardio: Acquisitions are one of the main ways that Chinese companies can become leaders. After I left *Business Week*, I was part of a National Academy of Science team that looked at innovation policy around the world. We did a trip to China. Everybody on this team, which consisted of academics and government officials, were trying to document China's awesome rise. By the end of a week, the conclusion was, they are spinning their wheels. This was the view of the Chinese, and the Academy of Sciences, and most of the government agencies and the companies that we talked to. Even ZTE said, "We're not catching up." There are a lot of reasons why it is dysfunctional when it comes applying all this engineering talent into true innovation and developing products that can be sold around the world.

The pattern today is that Chinese companies build large-scale presences in China and in other emerging markets. They get big enough that they take out the bottom part of the market. Then they attack the middle. The Chinese became leaders in the construction equipment industry this way, for example. Caterpillar is still bigger but Chinese companies are bigger than John Deere. After taking over the lower and middle segments of the industry, they started buying German companies that had great technology but couldn't stay in the game financially. This is the Chinese strategy.

It's also happening in lithium ion batteries. The U.S. government spent $2 billion subsidizing A123 Systems and other lithium ion battery makers. But the Chinese flooded the market with inexpensive photovoltaic cells. Now they are stepping up and buying the American companies, which were ahead by two generations in terms of technology, but they couldn't stay in the game financially. That's the strategy. They can do it in that sense.

Holstein: So you're something of a skeptic that the Chinese can emerge on their own steam, so to speak?

Engardio: Yes, I am something of a skeptic. You don't see a Chinese Toyota. The Chinese automakers are losing market share to the multinational brands in China. If the Chinese do make it to the top in a given industry, it will be through acquiring the technology.

Holstein to Schell: Is the American media doing a good job covering all this?

Schell: I think it's a fickle mistress. It's a tough one to cover. My bias is we've done a pretty reasonable job. The media has been a shrinking ice pad, slowing melting in the sun, as we all know. But by and large, the coverage has been pretty good. This is a very contradictory place where opposite things go in opposite directions and are true at the same time. It's very hard in circumstances like that to find a trend line. From my perspective, this is a system that shouldn't work. Who among us who stood in Tiananmen Square in 1989 and thought they would get this thing back together? Certainly no one in the media believed that. And yet they did. There are counter-intuitive things happening here, which has to make us all feel a bit chastened about our ability to judge. This is a country that's reinventing itself and adding lots of different elements. Actually, there is a kind of agility even though there is a tremendous rigidity as well as they put together whatever it is they're putting together to make this new economy, a new body politic, a new culture and a new value system.

Question and Answer Session:

Marcus Brauchli: On Pete's skepticism, I would just say that even though I agree with virtually everything he said, I would have trouble betting against 1.3 billion creative, increasingly well-educated people and expecting them not to figure out how to conquer industries. The question I want to ask John Bussey is, does China behave differently in terms of exercising regulatory influence over foreign companies than, say, European governments do?

Bussey: If you took the anti-monopoly law, you could say it's being used as a cudgel and as the latest thuggish romp by regulators or you could say it looks exactly what the European Union did its own anti-trust laws or what the U.S. did in 1890 with the Sherman Anti-Trust Law.

Brauchli: In that case, we were picking on our own companies. Europe has used its anti-trust laws to develop national champions.

Bussey: Yes, the Chinese have cited the European experience in writing their own anti-trust laws. But it's not just that law. It's the accumulation of regulatory tools and intrusions—standards setting that foreign companies can't meet, but domestic companies can meet. Indigenous innovation requirements that you need to transfer technology to the country if you are going to get a deal. You're going to have to team up with a local partner. You can't go it alone. All of the things that companies have had to endure over the past 20 years that lead to the feeling that regulators are intruding in an effort to build national champions. But can you blame China? Can you blame China for wanting to be able to circumvent the licensing fees of Microsoft or whoever? They realize they are what they are, which is fertile ground and undeveloped. If it were Americans doing this to prevent foreign companies from overwhelming our market, would we be so outraged?

Question from former OPC President Allan Dodds Frank: The Federal Bureau of Investigation just brought a case in Pittsburgh about industrial intellectual property being stolen by the Chinese. Is there any indication anywhere that the main industries and leadership in China are going to change course or are they going to continue that practice?

Schell: All of us in the field in China can feel that pressure, which has to be exerted on a question like Intellectual Property. But the Chinese are much more resistant to whatever kind of pressure is brought to bear. Gone are the days when an American president goes to China and dissidents get released. I think this is also true in lobbying for very hard, cold economic interests. The pressure is often counter-productive. I think we are going to have increasing difficulty making our case in whatever area it is because of this confidence, which is in many ways born out of a sense of weakness. But it is more and more rigid and more and more resistant. It means that the dynamic between us and them is changing quite rapidly and it is going to make it much more difficult in whatever field of endeavor you're in to push and get results.

Holstein question to Jamie Florcruz: How long have you been in China and what is your perspective on all this?

Florcruz: I arrived in 1971 and have lived there since except for one year. How do we explain China's ability to emerge from what many of us thought was the wreckage in the 1970s? They used to be obsessed with class struggle and soon after Mao Tse-tung died in 1976, they snapped out of it and unlike the former Soviet Union, they managed to pick up where they left off in 1949 and move on to market-oriented reforms. I think we may be underestimating the resilience of the Chinese in coping with these cycles of crisis upon crisis. I never expected China to be what it is now and neither did Orville. After 1989 (the Tiananmen massacre), I remember speaking to the Los Angeles Council on Foreign Affairs. I said I thought the Chinese could muddle through post-1989 and survive, and they have.

My question is this: I heard the Chinese are quite keen to join the Trans-Pacific Partnership free trade negotiations. (They have been excluded from talks that include Singapore, Japan, the United States and other countries of Southeast Asia.) My source in Beijing says it will change China even more if they get into it. I don't know whether Xi would use that as his next way to push China further into the world system and also to change the way things are done in China. Has anyone heard this and how significant might it be?

Bussey: One question is whether China wants to be part of this TPP and is in fact is using Singapore and other proxies in the negotiations to try to torpedo conditions that would make it impossible for China to join in the future. Then there is another case that, in this one instance, China and Japan have interests in common, to use gaiatsu, or foreign pressure, to make changes internally. There is also a bilateral investment treaty between China and the United States that would do much the same thing. They would use these negotiations to force change on the state-owned enterprises, to limit the state's percentage of ownership or to let the currency float or a variety of different issues. My suspicion is it's probably what you describe—some of this is being floated to help Xi force the changes that he wishes to make economically domestically.

Holstein: My view is that the time is not right for any kind of free trade negotiations. They have to get approved at some point and our political system at the moment is paralyzed. The entire climate of U.S. opinion is not ready for a big new free trade deal.

Bussey: I would disagree with that because deals with Korea and Columbia went through. After these elections, you might see some movement on trade promotion authority.

-0-

Subsequent commentary:

Keith Bradsher, in *The New York Times* on Nov. 10, 2014, wrote: "China is changing the rule book for business, forcing multinational companies to figure out how to play a new game or risk losing out on the world's second largest economy.

"When China joined the World Trade Organization 13 years ago, the government welcomed foreign companies, eager for their factories and technology. Now China is using its growing economic and financial muscle to dictate new terms, as dozens of American, European and Japanese businesses face scrutiny for corruption, monopolistic practices and, most recently, tax evasion."

PANEL 2

Covering the Contradictions of Today's China

Human rights, protests and an authoritarian government are all hot-button U.S. media issues. But how do we address the life of China's middle class; very real gains in open society and the media environment; and the emergence of a civil society in the environment and the arts?

MODERATORS

Dorinda Elliott was based in China for *BusinessWeek* and *Newsweek* and was editor of *Asiaweek* in Hong Kong. She is currently editor and communications director at the Paulson Institute.

Marcus Brauchli was based in Hong Kong and Shanghai for *The Wall Street Journal* and rose to become managing editor of that paper before being named executive editor of the *Washington Post*.

PANELISTS

Barbara Demick, outgoing Beijing bureau chief of the *Los Angeles Times* and fellow at the Council on Foreign Relations.

Gady Epstein, Beijing bureau chief for *The Economist*. Epstein was hired by *The Economist* to help launch its China section after having served as the Beijing bureau chief for *Forbes* and the *Baltimore Sun*. He has lived in Beijing for more than 10 years.

Evan Osnos, former Beijing bureau chief for *The New Yorker* and author of *"Age of Ambition: Chasing Fortune, Truth and Faith in the New China."*

Elliott: What Marcus and I wanted to do was to talk about covering the contradictions of China. We're basically going to be provocateurs and hopefully come up with an interesting conversation about the prism through which we look at China. I think we've all had the experience of covering the story in depth and coming back to the States, where he hear the perception of our friends. They say it's a corrupt authoritarian country obsessed with economic growth, degraded by pollution and plagued by lots of human rights problems.

All those things are arguably true, but yet there is a huge nuance about what's going on there that touches on the question of why we all like being there. There is tremendous optimism. When you are on the ground, you might not feel it on a daily basis. But when you come in from outside, compared with the United States, you can feel this incredible optimism. Peoples' lives are basically improving in China. So are we getting the story right? Is there an issue with the way editors are playing the stories? Maybe the reporters who are doing the stories on the ground aren't doing the nuance stories because they don't get played prominently. So the question is, are we doing a good enough job of looking at what China is trying to achieve from a Chinese perspective?

Epstein: I think that what people consume and what we produce are two very different things very often. When I talk to groups who come to Beijing, perhaps students or businessmen, if it's their first time, I often ask what their perceptions of China are before arriving. The answers haven't changed too significantly over time despite the fact that what we produce has expanded tremendously. China is one of the few places that there are more foreign correspondents on the ground than there were 10 or 20 years. The *Economist* added a China section. *Forbes*, my previous employer, added a Beijing bureau. I think there's a lot of nuance but it doesn't always penetrate readers who are watching TV or watching Jon Stewart. We care a lot about the nuance of the story and we do present it.

Osnos: There is a collective wisdom about China that takes hold in the United States. This is not unique to China. If we were having a conversation about coverage of France, there would be questions about whether the media gets it right.

French audience participant, Nicolas Becquelin, from Human Rights Watch: Non! (Laughter)

Osnos: Three years ago, I was at a conference where we were having a China panel and we were asked to give our sense of what was going on. At the time, I was working on a story about corruption. This was a business audience. I gave a talk about the Wenzhou train crash. That crash in the Chinese mind was really about corruption. It was about the government losing its sense of what its people wanted and about a sense that the government was not responding to them. That's what it meant to the Chinese ear.

But there was a lot of hostility from people in the audience who had investments in China. There were a lot of reasons why people did not want to hear that corruption was becoming a story.

A year later, China declared that corruption a big problem and a story. And all of a sudden American perception shifted. A year later, I went back to the same group and we had another panel. Afterward, everyone was saying "China is done. We're getting out of China. China is finished." I found myself in the unlikely position of saying, "Actually, there is a lot of really good stuff going on there. You don't want to abandon China." To me, it's not that we're stuck in a single frame. It's more that we have a tendency for to swing from one pole to another pretty dramatically.

Demick: The basic problem is that nuance doesn't sell. People don't like nuance. They want things to be very good or very bad. I've found this to be true of every country I've covered. I started as a foreign correspondent covering the Bosnian war. When it was the bad Serbs against good Muslims, the story was great. But when the Croats came in and things got complicated, with three sides involved in the fight, it fell from the front page to A16 and B32 and off the map. I've been told that the stories that sell are those that confirm a stereotype like, Chinese food is tainted. Or defy a stereotype: the French are getting fatter. These stories are the link bait that people go for. I don't think it's a unique problem to China.

Elliott: Let's talk about our prisms. I went scrolling through the stories about the Uighur attacks in Kunming. The Chinese saw that as their version of Sept. 11. It was very traumatic. The Chinese are very conscious of the fact that some Western coverage refers to the Uighurs as "terrorists" in quotation marks, which absolutely outraged the Chinese. They felt these people were terrorists. We all know that one man's terrorist is another man's freedom fighter. We in the Western press see the problems in Xinjiang and know that the Uighurs in Xinjiang are incredibly unhappy for very good reason, but how do we play a terrorist attack? Why should that word be in quotation marks?

Demick: I heard from people at the State Department that the U.S. kind of screwed up on this one. They was a lot of reluctance to call this a terror attack because the Chinese have so often given out dodgy information about these attacks. You have a criminal gang with knives and they get into a fight with police.

Someone finds a Koran and suddenly they were all jihadists. So the United States had a very slow reaction, as did journalists. But the closer you look at it, civilians were killed for political motives. It was a terrorist attack. Subsequently, there was a terrorist attack in Urumqi in June and the U.S. called it a terrorist attack. And so did we. But in general, I try to avoid using the word "terror" because it is so loaded.

Epstein: Bringing it back to the China versus the rest of the world perspective, I think after a major terror attack in the Middle East, you don't have hundreds of reporters on the ground who are specialists on the topic. In China, you do. You already have a case in which people can explain why it happened and present the context instead of just presenting the big news story and the reactions. It's sometimes perceived that we are trying to paper over a terrorist incident with nuance when actually we're just providing deeper reportage.

Osnos: I think there is a mechanical problem in the reporting experience about Xinjiang in that we can't go there very easily. As a journalist, when you're deprived of access, you become skeptical. It's hard to convey that in a story, particularly a short story. You're trying to explain something quickly. You're trying to explain that there is a pattern of behavior on the part of these militants, these terrorists, and also explain that there are domestic reasons this is happening. You can't go there to interview the people involved. Our default position is to be skeptical, to be slow, until we see something that persuades us that this is the right narrative. I think this is one of the reasons why the writing about Tibet and Xinjiang is so skeptical.

Brauchli: Barbara, you said that nuance doesn't sell. How big an issue is this for all you? To what extent is it possible that editors expect and want and how they play stories. Can it affect your coverage and skew your coverage in some way?

Epstein: At the *Economist*, when we started the China section, we had a lot of discussion about how to portray China. It comes up on almost every big story. You can do them in diametrically opposing ways. We did a big feature on NGOs (non-governmental organizations) earlier this year that was quite optimistic that we could easily have done in exactly the opposite way. At the moment, we would have looked a lot better if we did it in the negative way. Last year, we did a story on land reform that was quite optimistic. There are a lot of experiments in China going on related to land reform. You also can argue that for most rural Chinese, their situation won't change over the next decade and their land will continue to be seized by local officials in most cases. We could have presented it in the opposite way.

I also did a story last year about the massive 75 percent decline in death penalties and executions over the past decade. But we could have said that China executes 85 percent of the people who are executed in the world and how awful that is. This is true of every story. With China, there is a view of it as being a society and a state in transition. It's not decided yet where it's headed and we're allowed to project more hopes and fears on it than we are on a more developed country, like France.

Demick to Osnos: If you pitch a story to (*New Yorker* editor) David Remnick and say, well, the situation is not that bad, you're going to have a hard time to get him to want the story, right?

Osnos: *The New Yorker* is a weird place. We do stories that are longer. They are structurally designed to have nuance. If you don't have nuance, it's hard to write 10,000 words about anything. Previously, I worked for the *Chicago Tribune* in China for three years. The truth is that in a single Chinese life you do encounter the full range of things we're talking about. It's more satisfying as a story. You can write about someone who made their pot of gold as a dumpling plutocrat and then became politically active individual. You can get both of those in the same longer piece. It's harder to do that in a shorter format.

And yes, sometimes editors want to drive sales. The only time I've been advised to move in that direction was when I was doing a project about religion and Christianity in China. I had wooly ideas about what we should call the story. But the editors decided they were going to call it "Jesus in China." I asked, why are we going to do that. I was told, "if we put Jesus in the title, everything else is going to be gravy." (Laughter.)

Brauchi: What stories about China are undercovered or are hard to sell in the outside world?

Epstein: I think the human rights story is very hard to sell. Because I think people have gotten tired of it over the past 10 or 15 years. There is a lot more going on than we write about. The Gao Zhisheng case gets written about a little bit when there's a big development, but day by day, there are a lot of lawyers being put behind bars. You see maybe a story in the *Guardian* or maybe the *Times of London* will do a brief about it. It doesn't get the kind of extensive coverage it would have in an another era, before China joined the World Trade Organization.

Brauchli: Is it because the U.S. government is less focused on it and doesn't have as much leverage as it had before China joined the WTO?

Epstein. Right. We don't have the high profile prisoner diplomacy going on now. That doesn't happen. It's a

39

combination of reader fatigue, journalist fatigue and editor fatigue. Because the story is relentless.

Elliott: It's your job to make sure your coverage is comprehensive and your readers get a good sense of all the facets of China. Do you think that through? Do you say, over the next year, here are the topics I want to make sure my readers know about? On one hand, you have the new urbanization and the government is looking at environmental issues for the first time seriously. You've got human rights activists, people in the NGO world, and a lot of great stuff going on an individual basis. Yet at the same time, political reform is not the goal of President Xi Jinping, as Orville Schell said at lunch. He sees the Communist Party as China's salvation. That raises interesting questions for us as journalists. We're constantly fighting against that position as journalists, as opposed to saying perhaps that's just the way China is. Xi Jinping is looking at the big picture and saying the individual be damned. It's a huge ship and we're headed in that direction. So how do you figure out what your balance should be?

Osnos: One's assessment of China is a very imprecise instrument, but you have to ask, is my image of the country up-to-date and is the image I'm projecting in my coverage up-to-date? This is the weird thing about journalism—we have no hard metric to analyze our performance. I was a reporter Iraq in the early days of the war. And the military was constantly saying to us, "You're being too negative about the war." And we'd say, "Some things are going right but a lot of things are going wrong." They'd come back and say, "We did a measurement and 70 percent of your stories are about things going wrong." I remember thinking, actually, 70 percent of the war *is* really going wrong. (Laughter.) But we don't have data and when it comes to China, it's even harder. If you're writing five long pieces a year and you've got to get the right proportion in one year, you write two stories that are about bad things, two stories about good things and one story asking, "Who the hell knows what's going on here?" It's a mixed picture.

Epstein: We make that calculation in the China Section on a weekly basis. If, for three weeks in a row, the story has gone extremely political, then a story that has a soft, human individual kind of focus will have a much better chance of rising to the top. I did a story once about an activist in a village who happened, against all the odds, to be able to bring about change in his village. That's not what usually happens to the village activist, but we wrote about how it could be done. That was a lead piece in our China section one week. But it doesn't paint the whole picture. Talking about what Xi is trying to do, or the crackdown on lawyers, or whatever is necessary to balance that, you wing it on a week by week basis. As Evan says, it's a very imprecise measurement. Covering China is a lot writing about long geological eras. Gordon Chang wrote the "Coming Collapse of China" in 2001 and I'm convinced that in the year 2050, he'll be seen as a genius. People will say, "He saw it 30 years in advance." But for a long time, between now and then, he's not going to seem like a genius.

Elliott: Do you all think the coverage of hacking and cyber spying has been fair and balanced?

Demick: It's a tough story for us to cover. Most of the coverage originates out of Washington.

Elliott: That may be part of the problem. When I'm reading a cyber spying story, I'm always feeling, "What about the other side?" The big story is essentially there is a cyber war underway. Both sides are desperately trying to spy on each other. Seeing a front-page story strategically leaked to the Washington bureau of a newspaper about the U.S. discovering China's cyber spying, I'm always wondering about the other side.

Demick: Whenever there is an allegation out of Washington, there is an outraged editorial in the *Global Times* (an official Chinese newspaper) about what the Americans are doing. Because the coverage is bifurcated. I don't see many people weighing in trying to answer which side doing worse things.

Elliott: Could there be a better mechanism for you to get both sides of the story?

Osnos: If you were a reporter in Beijing and the Chinese government said to you, "We want to leak to you information about U.S. cyber spying," we would race over there because that would be a fabulous story. But it isn't going to happen. The other reason why we don't always achieve parity in our coverage is that there is a distinction between what the Chinese and Americans are doing. The Chinese are stealing commercial secrets from American companies to get commercial advantage for Chinese companies whereas the National Security Agency is systematically trying to break into the Chinese government's computers.

Brauchli: Having been an editor in New York and Washington, I think China doesn't help its credibility with the way it behaves toward journalists. What we often times don't get at is, what is China's real thinking and what are the real actions? It's difficult to understand to what extent their spying is centrally driven as opposed to being driven by various other organizations. They are really lousy at telling, with any credibility, what the United States might be doing to them. I felt for a long time when we ran lots of stories about Chinese spying on American companies that there must be something going the other way.

Then we got the revelations from Mr. (Edward) Snowden. It is not all government-to-government. The U.S. government, for example, was planting chips in computers that were being sold to Chinese companies. One of the responsibilities that the U.S. press has is try to make China's case for it because it won't make it for itself. Somehow we have to come to some understanding. As with North Korea, the temptation has always been to portray various Kims who run North Korea as madmen who act arbitrarily and without any real rationale. But the secret to writing about North Korea is understanding what their reasoning is because inevitably there is some sort of reasoning and rationale. It's much the same with China. China, of course, is a lot more open in some ways. But understanding what is going on in the Chinese government and what they are trying to accomplish is one area where we have to more on behalf of China. They are not going to do it themselves.

Elliott: I'm wondering whether part of the problem is the nature of television coverage of China. As we were saying earlier, we're writing the nuance but people aren't hearing it. I have a story here that was written by NBC News about charges that China was targeting six American companies. The NBC story never mentions Snowden and his revelations. Other stories from the *New York Times, Washington Post,* and *Los Angeles Times* buried the complexity caused by Snowden's revelations but it was in the story. But NBC said only that the Chinese are bad guys and they are targeting our companies.

Epstein: When it comes to commercial secrets, there is a lot more for the Chinese to steal, on an exponential scale, than over what there is for America to try to steal from Chinese companies.

There is an imbalance there. But to expand on the point on why people are consuming only a layer of the story, it's not so much TV these days than it is Twitter with 140-character messages, and Facebook and headlines. Who's actually reading any of those stories? They're clicking on pet cat videos.

Demick: A lot of those 140-character assessments about what's going on in China are just wrong. There was a story I was trying to chase down about two years ago, "China just bought 5 percent of the Ukraine." It was good "link bait" but when you got into the nuance it turned out that there was a long-term lease on a sizable tract of land and it could go up to a certain amount.

Osnos: One thing we haven't talked about in the role of the foreign press in China over the last few years is that we are now writing partly for a Chinese audience. This is important. If you look at the work that the *New York Times* and Bloomberg did about the private wealth of the Party's leadership, and you can argue the same thing about writing about human rights abuses, there is a special responsibility for the foreign press to write about things that the Chinese press is either legally or practically prevented from writing about. In our overall mix, we probably have more stories exposing things in China.

Elliott: There's a long tradition of the press covering dissidents. It's a very important tradition. From a purely journalistic point of view, these are the people pushing for change and that by definition makes them interesting. They are agents trying to move their society forward. I'm sure you wrestle a lot with the how much coverage of that you provide.

One last question before we jump to the audience, we were talking at lunch about the anti-monopoly law situation in China. There was a discussion of how Europe also uses anti-monopoly laws to allow the development of their companies. Do we lose nuance by suggesting China is alone in doing this? It's just part of their strategy. Is there a reason why we should do a better job of explaining it with a little broader perspective?

Epstein: You have to base it on what evidence you're getting in each case. Our responsibility is to be rigorous when we write our stories. I've been hearing from business people and colleagues that when some Western companies go in for these meetings with Chinese authorities, the Chinese side is saying, "We have you over a barrel. You know what you did. Don't hire a lawyer." There is no presentation of evidence. All of these things are not the rule of law. If the proceedings are like that, they are quite scary and we have a responsibility to present that.

Question from Bill Holstein: Regarding the underlying assumptions about where China is headed, we've heard a lot about China being in flux and it's too hard to tell where it's going. We in the media still seem to talk about how pluralism is going to break out, how the emerging middle class is going to demand more involvement in decision-making, how a legal system is going to be born, and how a civil society is going to be established at some level. But it seems the story is not going that way under Xi Jinping. What are the assumptions that shape our coverage and at what point do we say, "This is what we see happening on the ground, ladies and gentlemen, and it doesn't seem to be working out the way we had envisioned it."?

Epstein: You're quite right. It would be humbling to go back and look at stories from 10 years ago or 20 years ago that talked about reforms that were going on regarding legal system or the creation of a civil society. It would be quite humbling. All you can do is present it this way: "Okay, here is what they say they're trying to do. But here is the historical context of what actually has happened." Then the question is how the story is received by the reader depending on what weight you give those variables." I would weight the coverage more in the direction of, "Don't be too optimistic that anything is going to be transformed in the next few years. It is going to be a long, slow slog. Meanwhile, perhaps hundreds of millions of people won't be seeing any benefits of reforms for some years to come. We don't know what it will look like in 10 years. I don't think I would be writing any stories about political pluralism these days.

Osnos: I think we're at this interesting moment. There was a book that James Mann wrote a few years ago (in 2008) called "The China Fantasy" which got to the heart of this question. For years, he said, we've been operating on the presumption that as China becomes more prosperous and more integrated with the rest of the world, this will necessarily lead to the kind of institutions and political culture that we recognize. But he said, "It's time to call our own bluff. It's not happening." He was right. It took us a while to absorb that idea and to then build it into our model of what that means for China. China has continued to re-integrate with the rest of the world at the same time that its political culture is moving in the opposite direction.

When you're covering China, there's a difference between declarations and facts on the ground. This is the biggest single collision between writers who live there and write about it all the time and people who come in occasionally and write about it. If you coming in from outside, you're much more likely to say, "The Chinese said there are going to build 10,000 windmills on the hills of Hubei." But if you live there and you go to Hubei, you find that 60 percent of them are not connected to anything and are just spinning around. Being on the ground, and not being captive to the proclamations and being faithful to the facts is harder than it sounds.

Epstein: To point out a case where I wasn't completely wrong, 10 years ago I did a series of stories about the rule of law based on the fact that they had added protections for human rights and private property to the constitution. Leaping from that, I went out to do some reporting and found a guy in Beijing whose property was being taken from him by the government. He didn't agree to any compensation. They just took him to the police station one morning and demolished his house. He came back to a demolished house. But he was a believer in the constitution. He protested what had happened for a couple of months. He stood on the rubble of his home with a copy of the constitution in his hand. It was a thing that year. There were people handing out copies of the new constitution and they were getting in trouble for it, of course. There were other defendants getting tortured even though the government had made a series of proclamations about how torture was illegal, but they were still torturing confessions out of defendants. So that's what we're talking about, "Here's what they are saying they're doing, but here's the reality on the ground and there is a very wide gulf between them."

This is actually true on all these issues they are talking about reforming, like land reform and hukou (the household registration system in which migrants from the countryside are denied privileges in major Chinese cities.) We've been hearing about household registration being phased out for a long time now and it's still going to be a long time. In the big cities where most of the migrants are, household registration is still going to be a fact for a very long time.

Demick: I think you have to look at the difference between what we traditionally think of as democratization, elections, civil society, pluralism, and freedom of the press and all that versus what is actually happening on the ground. I would argue there has been a lot of change. Not the big Capital R reform. But 30 percent of the people in Beijing do not have hukous. Kids who do not have hukous are able to go to schools in Beijing. I'm always amazed when I get out of Beijing and see how brave people are and how smart they are. There is a lot of change happening on the ground, but it's not in the format we might have expected.

Question from Nicolas Becquelin: I want to say this panel has deeply hurt the feelings of 60 million French people. (Laughter.)

I'd like to take the media off the hook here. It's not the quality of the reporting that is at the heart of the issue. I meet with diplomats and government officials all the time. We can take stacks of information that goes along with what we're trying to tell them. But they don't look at it. They look at other things. They look at the windmills in Hubei or whatever. For the general public and in the mind of policy-makers, especially in Europe, the problem is the Berlin Wall syndrome—they believe an authoritarian system can exist and in a single day it turns into a democracy. We're still looking at China in this way, waiting for that magic moment when it is going to suddenly flip. Every sign we interpret as meaning, "Yes, the country is going down the road of democratization. Or else we say, no, this is the opposite. They want more authoritarianism."

The reality is that there is no historical precedence for what we are seeing in China today. There is no political science model we can apply. We just have to take it as it is. We are still prisoners of this 1989 mindset (when the Berlin Wall fell). If you look at China, and think of the Berlin Wall, it doesn't work. But if you look at China and see the "Age of Ambition," you get a much better sense of where China is at today. That's what Chinese leaders are thinking about. How we do we fulfill our ambitions? Are they giving themselves the means to achieve the goals they have set for themselves?

Pete Engardio: You see a lot of skirmishes now with people taking on authorities over various things. Sometimes they win and sometimes they lose. Maybe that's progress. But at an institutional level, are you seeing any real change in the legal system and the court system? It looks like they seem to be rounding up every important human rights attorney and putting them in the gulag right now. So my question is, is there real progress being made in the legal system?

Jerome Cohen, co-director, U.S.-Asia Law Institute, New York University School of Law: Contradiction is the right term for what's taking place in the legal system. They're gradually making better laws. That's progress. And the view of Chinese law professors who are helping on this, and they're very influential, is that these norms will be implemented to a greater extent. But they're afraid to worry about practice. They want to keep their jobs so they usually keep their silence. Lawyers occasionally will speak out despite the controls of the Party and the Ministry of Justice, which is waging a tremendous campaign against them now.

Practice is going the other way (against Western-style reforms), as was already recognized here. You have a high degree of repression of lawyers. It's so different from 10 years ago when people were predicting great things would happen in practice as well as legislation. So the gap is really increasing between better pieces of paper and the hideous practice with respect to many things.

There are lots of mundane cases, hundreds of thousands, where things are being carried on in an acceptable way. But there are hundreds of thousands, not just a few politically sensitive cases, where they're not. The system is under enormous tension. There are institutional changes underway in the relationship of the Party to the formal government legal system.

But they are very obscure, very hard to see. The will of the center (the central government in Beijing) is not being implemented in a consistent, uniform way throughout the country. There is an ongoing struggle. But the Party is going to continue to control the legal system. The meeting of the Fourth Plenum next month (October 2014), which will talk about the rule of law, is really an attempt by the central government to enforce its will over the localities. They want to stop courts from being influenced by local factors. They want to make sure courts aren't really independent but are responsive exclusively to the will of the center.

Zhou Yongkang, when he was minister of public security, tried very hard to get the ministry to control better what was taking place on the ground. He made some progress but not enough. That's why they are trying to curb the influence of corruption, local protectionism, neighbors' interests, and all the things that distort a court's judgment. They are trying to move the real influence up higher so that it isn't the locality that's appointing judges, or deciding how much to pay them, or whether they're going be removed, or determining the court budget. They'd love it for the center to control all this, but the center can't really do the job. So it's at the provincial level that there's a struggle now.

But the terrible thing is what's been happening to lawyers, who are where the rubber meets the road. They are the ones who try to apply these norms. And they're the ones who have been more repressed. You wonder why there are still lawyers fighting the fight. The *Sunday Times of London* ran an article about Gao Zisheng and asked, "Is he coming back?" My question is: Is he a vegetable? In 2006, I told Gao, "If you keep this up, you're not gonna be on the street." But he spoke the truth. And they broke him even though he was so proud and almost arrogant. He thought they couldn't break him.

I keep holding out Japan to them as a model. Japan has judicial independence. But they have a lot of control of the judiciary from the central secretariat. And if a judge makes the wrong decision, he won't be in Tokyo much longer even though he'd like to be. They'll move him out to some remote island. They have their own ways, but it looks a lot better and it is a lot better in practice. That would be a good model for China. But they're not ready for the Party to tolerate autonomous decisions.

Epstein: I, of course, agree with Jerry on all of that. I think the framework for thinking about rule of law reform or other areas of Chinese governance—take the Internet, for instance—is that they want to become smarter at being authoritarian. There's no question of them liberalizing politically. It's a matter of doing things that make them better at being an authoritarian government.

Tim Ferguson, *Forbes Asia*: Would you say that respectable journalists in China share the same compass or consciousness? Or is there room for fundamental disagreement?

Epstein: Even within *The Economist*, there are people who see reforms optimistically, or on the other hand pessimistically, or cynically, or realistically, or however you want to describe it. There is definitely a variety of perspectives. At times, it leans heavily towards one direction or the other.

Osnos: Ten years ago, I would have conversations with a business audience in which it tended to be that people who were doing business in China were much more positive about the country. They were the ones who were saying, "Well, you're overlooking this," and, "This is the good side."

Something has moved there. In Washington these days, the community that used to be the most stalwart defenders of China in Congress is a little bit more conflicted about that now particularly in private but increasingly in public, too. From a diplomatic perspective, once China loses the U.S. business lobby, they're really in a difficult position.

Demick: I was just going to follow up on something that Evan said earlier—that we're much more writing for a Chinese audience. That's something that's changed, just in the seven years that I was in Beijing because of the Internet. When we're sometimes in very obscure places writing about whether it's family planning, or lead poisoning, or corruption in railroad ticket sales, ordinary people, not necessarily English speakers, are reading our stuff or Chinese language versions of our stuff. Or if they're not reading it, somebody they know is. In every village, there is some kid who's made good, who's gone to Guangzhou and has the iPhone or the Galaxy. The Chinese are somehow looking to us and the foreign press to write stories for them. I've had many, many situations where I've gone into a village and people have said, "Thanks for reporting that story for the Chinese people."

Elliott: Those must be great, great moments when you get that reflected back to you and you feel like maybe you're actually doing the right thing. Maybe your coverage is hitting the right notes. We've been very lucky today to have some of the best journalists who have been covering China over the past decade and more. Thank you so much for joining us.

-0-

Subsequent commentary:

Gordon Crovitz, writing an opinion piece in the *Wall Street Journal* on Oct. 5: "Mainland China is in an era of brutal suppression. Beijing jails reformers, controls journalists and employs hundreds of thousands of censors on social media. Twitter, Facebook, YouTube and many global news sites are blocked. Instagram was closed down after mainlanders shared photos of Hong Kong people using umbrellas against pepper spray and tear gas."

Evan Osnos, writing in Oct. 13 issue of *The New Yorker*: "Resolving the (Hong Kong) crisis falls to President Xi Jinping, in Beijing. Eighteen months after taking office, the tall, phlegmatic son of the Communist aristocracy has swiftly consolidated control of the Party and the military, arresting thousands of officials in an anti-corruption campaign and promoting his personal brand of power. For years, Beijing has downplayed the importance of any single leader, for fear of creating another cult of personality. Xi is reversing that trend: he has already graced the pages of the *People's Daily* more times than any leader since Chairman Mao; last week, the government issued a book of his quotations in nine languages.

"Xi sanctifies absolutism as a key to political survival...He has staked his presidency on a 'great renewal' of China, a nationalist project that leaves little room for regional identities. Last year, when the Party faced mounting complaints over deadly air pollution, Internet censorship, and rampant graft, it arrested lawyers, activists, and journalists in the harshest such measures in decades, and circulated an internal directive to senior members. The notice identified seven 'unmentionable' topics: Western-style democracy, universal values, civil society, pro-market liberalism, a free press, 'nihilist' criticisms of Party history, and questions about the pace of China's reforms."

Nicholas Kristof, writing an op ed article in *The New York Times* on Nov. 9, 2014: "...President Xi Jinping is tugging his regime in a more nationalistic, assertive and hard-line direction...Xi has been ruling China for two years now, and he has shown some inclination toward economic and legal reforms. Two years ago, I thought Xi might open things up a bit. Boy, was I wrong! Instead, it increasingly seems that Xi may deepen reforms in some areas but, overall, is a tough-minded nationalist who takes a hard line on multiple fronts so as the challenge nearly everything that (President) Obama stands for."

PANEL 3
Chinese Government Crackdown on Western Media

The Foreign Correspondents Club of China released its latest findings on how the government is trying to squeeze the Western press.

MODERATOR

Jocelyn Ford, representing the Foreign Correspondents Club of China.

PANELISTS

Kathleen McLaughlin, a Knight Science Journalism fellow at MIT, China/Asia contributor to *The Economist* and the *Guardian*, and former China correspondent for Global Post/PBS NewsHour and Bloomberg BNA.

Joseph Kahn, former Beijing correspondent and currently foreign editor of *The New York Times*.

Minky Worden, director of global initiatives, Human Rights Watch.

Ford: The Foreign Correspondents Club of China is very pleased to be here. And it is fortuitous that this is the very week that we finished our first, comprehensive report summarizing all of the barriers we face as foreign correspondents in China, with 29 recommendations for the Chinese government to take action on.

We have a distinguished panel of people today who have been on the ground and faced many of the issues that are spoken about in the report. I'll get to them in a minute. But I first wanted to give a little bit of background about how the Foreign Correspondents Club became engaged in monitoring the reporting situation. Around 2005, we started what was essentially a press freedoms committee. We then called it the Professional Committee to avoid alarming Chinese authorities about what we were doing. We started surveying our members about the sorts of obstacles they faced when they go out in the field. I helped start the questionnaire and have been involved in it ever since. Now it's become an annual survey.

At the start, I had a huge difficulty because I would ask my colleagues, "Okay, have you faced any obstacles?" And people would say, "Oh, I went to such-and-such village and they kicked me out. But it's China."

I found that the biggest job I had was to try to encourage my colleagues to *not* give China a break. China did not deserve an exception. China was going to become a very important country and we should at least start establishing a gold standard.

Without further ado, I will turn it over to Kathleen McLaughlin, who's another former head of the Press Freedoms Committee. She arrived in Shanghai in 2002 and was there until 2007. Then she started reported from Beijing in 2008. She has reported for everyone under the sun, such as *The Economist, The Guardian*, and others. Kathleen has just returned to the U.S. where she is starting a fellowship at M.I.T., in Cambridge, Ma.

McLaughlin: I have to credit Jocelyn because she's done a tremendous job in educating foreign correspondents on what constitutes interference. I think a lot of us are willing to say, "Oh, it's China. Of course, an unmarked car is going to follow you while you're reporting in Hubei." But, actually, it shouldn't be that way.

In 2008, you're probably all aware that China enacted new reporting regulations for foreign correspondents in China. They were meant to open up the field and provide foreign correspondents in China with more opportunities in the run up to the Beijing Olympics.

Unfortunately, after the Olympics that year, we began to see a backslide. And in the years since, we have seen increasing losses in what we're able to cover, in new regional restrictions, and in new policies that prevent foreign journalists from being able to cover the world's second-largest economy openly. I'm sure that many of you who were there a long time ago think that, well, it's better than it was when we were there. That's absolutely true.

But the fact is, China wants to be a major player in the world and we should have the same kind of access to China that we have to any other country under international standards. But the latest Foreign Correspondent Club of China survey indicated that 99% of our members do not believe that China meets international standards for reporting conditions, which means that only 1% believe it does.

The No. 1 area we have flagged for action is restrictive reporting conditions. It's been getting worse. In our latest survey, two-thirds of journalists who responded said they've experienced interference, harassment, or violence while attempting to report in China in the previous year. Among those, 10% were subjected to manhandling or physical force.

Other forms of interference and restrictions are growing. Certain events have become hot spots for correspondents to be arrested, threatened, and manhandled. There's been a growing trend of preemptive interference in coverage as when the authorities called correspondents up and said, "Don't go to Tiananmen Square on June 4" (the anniversary of the 1989 crackdown).

That's become pretty commonplace and troubling. Tiananmen is not officially off-limits to anyone and that includes foreign correspondents. Cyber attacks continue against reporters and media companies. And there does appear to be a new and growing campaign by Chinese officials to pressure their journalists about coverage from outside of China. We've had several major news organizations from Europe and the U.S. report that embassy staff in their home countries visited their headquarters complaining about stories they didn't write.

The second area where we want action is our news assistants. We're only as good as our Chinese staff and our Chinese staffs have been coming under increasing pressure. Half of the correspondents who have a news assistant said that their news assistant was harassed or intimidated at least once in the last year. That's up from 35% the year before.

The third area, and possibly more important category than the first two, is the harassment of sources. We should be able to interview Chinese sources without them fearing reprisals or repercussions. Increasingly, that's just not the case. One example from the survey—one European television reporter said, "After visiting a village for a story on family planning, all of our sources were contacted by police and state security and issued stern warnings. One source was told, 'You know, you can lose your life for talking to a foreign journalist.'"

That's the environment that we are reporting in. If people who talk to us can't expect to remain safe, they're not going to want to talk to us.

A fourth area of concern is the denial of access to government information. That includes new classification of data and other materials to make them considered to be "state secrets." This is a growing trend, particularly with economic data that was once public.

But also now, Chinese journalists have been issued a directive to not share information about their work with foreign journalists. So you can no longer go for coffee or a drink with a Chinese journalist and talk about stories and share ideas and sources, according to this regulation. That's not a good situation.

The fifth area of concern is denial of access to the Chinese market. It's become increasingly clear that your website will be blocked in China if you write something the government doesn't like. So that's happened to several news organizations in the past few years, after investigative reporting in China. That's a pretty clear business issue.

The sixth big issue, which I think Joe Kahn will go into in detail, is punitive visa policies. In 2014, 18% of the respondents had difficulty renewing their press cards or visas. Among those, half said that they were threatened over specific coverage. So China is using the visa and the press card as a lever. As you know, there have been several high-profile expulsions. Delays have become commonplace. In contrast, that isn't a problem for Chinese journalists reporting in the U.S. or in most other open countries.

So it is a very specific thing that China is doing to control access to information. As a result, global coverage of China has been hindered. A couple of other issues I'm just going throw in at the end. One is online media. China does not officially recognize online media as media. I tried for three-and-a-half years to get a license and a press card for the online news site, *GlobalPost*, first through *GlobalPost* alone and then under the banner of the PBS *NewsHour*. Neither one was ever granted. To this day, only one online news organization has been able to get a visa, which was a six-month, temporary visa. It was not even a resident press card.

The second additional issue is freelancers. Freelancers have been in the news lately for very tragic reasons in Syria. We all need to remember that there are freelancers in China also who are skirting legal regulations to be there because China doesn't recognize freelance journalists either. Hopefully, you all here today can help us come up with some ideas on how to make the situation better, going forward. Thanks very much.

Ford: Thank you, Kathleen. The full paper, consisting of 14 pages, is available online in the Foreign Correspondents Club press site and the OPC will release it on their website as well (www.opcofamerica.org.) Joe Kahn first was in Beijing in 1989 when he was working for the *Dallas Morning News*. He was then in Shanghai for the *Wall Street Journal* from 1993 to 1997, and *New York Times* from 2002 to 2008. He needs no further introduction.

Kahn: Unfortunately, I spend a lot of time talking about it because we at the *Times* are pretty solidly in the middle of many of the issues that the Foreign Correspondents Club of China is raising. Some of the problems date back to the 1970s when we first had correspondents in China. But the situation shifted pretty decisively on one particular day, which was October 25, 2012, when we published an article by David Barboza about the wealth of the family of Wen Jiabao, who was then in his final couple of months as China's prime minister.

The Chinese reaction to that story upended every assumption I had about the direction that we were moving in terms of China's treatment of the foreign media. The harassment, the intimidation of news assistants, the visa games that came up, the punishment of sources who spoke to international media were not unheard of.

But the kind of attitude that the Western media—particularly the two news organizations that published that kind of article—were fundamentally destructive to China's interests was new. It continues to be an unresolved problem.

There are a couple of reasons those stories had the impact they did. One is that the style of investigative reporting that David Barboza did came as something of a surprise to the Chinese. It was document-based research using not especially well-hidden Chinese records and documents about the securitization of all kinds of assets in China. It was fairly loosely disguised in terms of the ultimate ownership, sometimes using front companies.

But as David showed, and others have shown, it wasn't that difficult to unearth. It took effort, and it took lawyers acting as middlemen to get the records. But it wasn't an impossible task. I think there was a sharp reaction to the fact that there was all this documentation out there.

Secondly, I think the timing of the report, which came just before the 18th Party Congress, was a major factor in that it was seen as interference in China's internal political affairs and was viewed as an attempt to disrupt a once-in-five-year congress. We were viewed, as the Chinese view all American media, as an arm of the American government. It was seen as an American attempt to disrupt the political transition in China.

A third reason for their reaction is that because of the due diligence that we were doing on this story, we gave highlights of this story to a number of different government agencies and gave them time to respond. They responded very aggressively, including by sending a delegation to talk to our publisher and warn us of very specific consequences if we published the story. That didn't stop us from publishing the story. But it may have actually complicated the reaction to us. It might have been better if we had not gone through all that extra time and effort, which we knew was going to be useless anyway.

To get the no-comment reaction was unhelpful, even for the Chinese who on the whole would rather not have a war with the Western media. It was unhelpful because they stuck their necks out, making very strong threats to us, and then we did it anyway.

The final reason, as was mentioned earlier, is that back in the 1970s or '80s when you wrote harsh reports about repression in China or whatever, the damage was mainly to Western perceptions of China. But this report was pretty instantly available in Chinese partly because we translated ourselves and put it on our website. The story was very quickly was circulated around China.

So I think the distinction between something that was done by the Western media and something that was done by a misbehaving Chinese media started getting blurred in the official mind in China, and they reacted quite strongly. We've had a lot of dialogue with the Chinese government in the aftermath of that story.

My feeling is that their attitude has hardened quite a bit. There's been no sort of sign of understanding and no clear indication that there's a desire to move on and resume business as usual. We've had constant problems with visas and in fact those problems have intensified. We had a mini-drama at the end of last year where we were somewhat publicly threatened with having no visas for any of our resident correspondents, which would have meant eight or nine people needing to leave the country at the end of the year.

None of it was said formally. But nobody was getting their visa and we had people having to change and cancel their end-of-the-year vacation plans. After the intervention of Joe Biden, everybody got their visas.

But since then, even the sort of routine, temporary visas that we once applied for and got for correspondents outside of China who came in for very specific reporting purposes, or business meetings, or auto shows, or stuff that rarely results in what the Chinese see as objectionable coverage have also been withheld. Nick Kristof recently was supposed to be on a panel for the World Economic Forum in China. He had an official invitation letter and no real other reporting targets while he was in China. He was denied a visa. Our business correspondents in Hong Kong are now pretty systematically denied visas. So we don't really see the situation as softening up or improving.

You know, the foreign ministry never thanked Bloomberg or the *New York Times* for helping put corruption on the agenda. But the truth is that the issue is not as verboten as it seemed to be previously when the top leader (President Xi), perhaps in the course of consolidating power, or perhaps because he actually cares about the issue, is investigating and exposing wealth accumulation by the families of the military elite and the political elite.

At some point, there could be a helpful in softening in the Chinese position. These stories sort of play themselves out. They have a life cycle. The sort of investigative reporting about the financial holdings of relatives of members of the Politburo's Standing Committee are not going to be endlessly interesting to the outside world. It is not going to be anybody's sole line of coverage in a place as big, as important, as China. So the passage of time could help a little bit to sort of diversify the image that the official side in China has of the Western press.

In terms of the specific things that we, as a company, can do or we, as a collective Western media, can do, the simple answer is not a heck of a lot. We've gotten a very specific road map from the Chinese side as to what it would take to unblock our website and resume issuance of visas as usual. What it came down to was, "Don't publish stories we think are offensive, and you have to agree to do that in writing." (Laughter.) We're not going to do that. The *New York Times* is not a very big company anymore. It's dependent pretty much entirely on the journalism that we do. The moment that we even wink and nod that we're going to avoid a certain category of coverage or type of reporting in a place like China, I'm not sure what value our brand would have. So that's not an option for us and we've told them that.

The other option is to rely pretty heavily on the American government to go to bat for us. There are upsides and downsides to that. We consider ourselves independent from our own government. And we want to maintain some distance from whatever policy the government adopts in relation to visas. So we don't actually advocate a specific position and I don't think the company will. On the other hand, you know, we're regulated as journalists in China by the foreign ministry. They treat us as a diplomatic entity and they don't buy the line that we're not an agent of, broadly speaking, the American government.

So we really have no choice but to have the American government try to negotiate the visa issue—maybe also the website issue, as a matter diplomatic reciprocity, but also possibly trade reciprocity and market access. There's a debate going on within the (Obama) administration about whether to do this.

I hope that over time, some of the accumulated sort of frustrations about China that are also being felt in the business community, in the human rights community, among environmentalists, and in the legal community will lead to a little more pessimism about whether prosperity in China leads to greater openness. I hope that some of that accumulating pessimism ends up influencing the Chinese state of mind about the role of the Western media.

I don't think they're divorced from each other. It's possible that China will move from this kind of red light environment that we are seeing right now to a more sort of permissive and open phase at some point. But I don't dare pick a time when that might happen.

Ford: Thank you. I wish it had been more upbeat but that's the reality. We're always zigzagging through with China. Everything and its opposite exists. So we're on the bad zag at the moment, especially in Hong Kong. Our next speaker, Minky Worden, was in Hong Kong for most of the 1990s and is going to fill us in on what the recent trends are in the media in Hong Kong and the implications of this for the rest of the world.

Worden: First of all, I want to salute the Foreign Correspondents Club of China. You all have done an amazing thing. It's an important that this session has convened because it's an important and pivotal moment for press freedom in China. I do think that it is hard for individual news organizations who are negotiating visas and trying to keep their news assistants out of jail and even worse outcomes. I do think it's an important moment for the Foreign Correspondents Club of Hong Kong, the Foreign Correspondents Club of China, the Overseas Press Club, and other press freedom organizations, to speak with one voice.

I wanted to begin by asking for a show of hands in the room. How many of you were based in Hong Kong as foreign correspondents? (A majority of hands are raised.) That's pretty much everyone. A lot of the people who have covered China have, at times, covered it from Hong Kong. That is part of the importance of Hong Kong. It's an essential role that Hong Kong has played for many years. The good news is that 17 years after the handover (to China), Hong Kong is still relatively free.

Press organizations and new sites have prospered in ways that pessimists before and after 1997 (the handover year) thought might not be possible. That has been due to incredibly brave reporters, writers, editors, owners of newspapers. It's not due to the Chinese government letting people in Hong Kong have more press freedom.

The bad news is that in the past year, we've seen marked changes. We've seen ugly incidents, some of them without precedent in the 25 years I've been tracking events in Hong Kong. First of all, there's been censorship and sacking of critical reporters. There have been violent attacks on editors and the sacking of editors. Kevin Lau of *Ming Pao* is an example. Kevin Lau was not an incendiary figure. He was a very careful journalist and editor, the top editor of *Ming Pao*. But he was sacked this year and shortly thereafter was attacked with a chopper in broad daylight at around 10:00 a.m. He was nearly killed. The attempt was actually to cut him off at the legs, literally, so that he could not continue standing and reporting. That was shocking to people. The interesting thing is the reaction in Hong Kong. You had journalists and ordinary citizens marching in the street in support of press freedom.

It's still possible to do that. There is still the will to do that and that's very important.

I'd like to talk for a minute about another trend—the malevolent role of China's Central Liaison Office. It's not designed to be an office that you know about. But now they are calling up and are dictating, for example, to advertisers such as major multinational banks, including Citibank, the Bank of East Asia, and HSBC. The Central Liaison Office called up and asked them to pull their advertising from the *Apple Daily* group of papers, including *Next Magazine* and *Apple Daily*. These are very popular papers. But they're also critical of the Chinese government.

They're also quite critical of the Hong Kong government. The worst part of that story is that the banks did pull their advertising.

Anson Chan, the former chief secretary, wrote a letter to them asking them to explain this. The banks said that they had done so because of political considerations. They don't deny they did this. It's very straightforward.

The political climate in Hong Kong does affect the press freedom climate. Part of why we're seeing the tightening in Hong Kong, and threats to journalists and reporters, is that the news media has been covering democracy demands and the Occupy Central movement, which is demanding the democracy that was promised to Hong Kong people in international treaties.

The coverage of the democracy movement has led to a sense from the Chinese government that it wants to quash this coverage. The coverage is affecting votes. This past summer, there was an informal referendum. Some 800,000 people voted, saying they should be given the true vote they were promised in the joint declaration (between Britain and China), the basic law, and in other ways.

The joint declaration and the basic law are important documents. The joint declaration is a 1984 treaty that determined the handover of sovereignty from Hong Kong to China. It's registered at the United Nations. It's important because it requires the continued application of the international covenants regarding political rights to Hong Kong. That includes press freedom. So there's an international treaty protecting press freedom in Hong Kong. Hong Kong is in a fundamentally different situation from China. What's happening is, to use the Chinese expression, they are killing a chicken to scare the monkeys.

That's what the violent attacks on Kevin Lau and other editors have been. There was a case at *House News*, a online media site, where the editor was disappeared for three days, and came back, and *House News* is no more. That's an example of the Chinese government using the full range of tools at its disposal. But I think journalists in Hong Kong and those who support press freedom also have a full range of tools at our disposal.

The greatest friends of Hong Kong have been the journalists who have been based there. I really think that without them there would be very little coverage. It's a tiny territory. But there has been excellent coverage of what's happening in Hong Kong. So we're at a critical moment because the political fight is about to go into the streets.

There are threats to journalists. There are threats to news organizations. There are threats to owners. The international community and press freedom organizations have an essential role to play. If we can preserve and protect press freedom in Hong Kong, it's going to be a lot easier to improve it in China. Hong Kong is governed by these international treaties that expressly protect press freedom, and international governments such as the U.S. want to do the right thing. (I don't think we can look to the U.K. for anything and that's the bad news.) We're at a key moment for people to speak up about the situation in Hong Kong. Hong Kong's role as a global city where the free flow of information, including financial information, is important also gives us a piece of leverage.

So the situation in China is at probably the worst low since the post-1989 period. The situation in Hong Kong is probably the worst it's been since the handover in 1997. But there is reason for hope. I believe that if you can preserve press freedom in Hong Kong, you have a greater hope of seeing it in China in the future.

Ford: Joe, have there been efforts to among media organizations to collaborate in terms of dealing with these issues or does each organization take on its own battles?

Kahn: We haven't had a lot of attempts back here in the United States to come up with pan-U.S. media type of response. Part of the reason is that we're competitive with each other. While occasionally we do come to each other's aid on things like safety of journalists who are in a troubled spot, the divisions are probably more evident than the common ground on these sorts of issues. Even between Bloomberg and the *New York Times* there has been essentially no cooperation at all—and some hostility actually. We've had very different approaches to dealing with the problem. (Bloomberg has announced it will no longer pursue tough investigative stories in China to concentrate on expanding its business there.) News organizations that have correspondents in China and are getting visas don't have an overwhelmingly strong incentive band together with those that are having real problems and trying to put a great deal of pressure on the foreign ministry.

So there are some inherent contradictions among the news organizations that are there. What I pick up is that among the correspondents who are actually on the ground in China there's a lot more cooperation than there is at the headquarters level. In China, journalists are in the trenches together and communicate more. There's a natural sense of solidarity. The commonality comes from there as opposed to from here.

Ford: When I first arrived in China, one of the sayings from a colleague was, "We hang together or we hang apart." And I am afraid that we are feeling that our headquarters are hanging apart. That's causing difficulties on the ground.

McLaughlin: It was a very important step when the *New York Times* went public about what was happening because we at the FCCC have been tracking this visa issue since probably 2010. We knew this was happening. Our own visas got held up until the last hour just for being volunteer members of the FCCC board. But it didn't resonate back home until *The Times* went public. That was a really critical thing to do. It does make a difference in public perception. People are paying attention because I think there's a pretty widespread recognition of this problem now since *The Times* and Bloomberg went public with what was going on.

Worden: If the Chinese government is going to use the classic united front tactic (a long-term strategy in which a target is encircled and slowly squeezed from all directions) against journalists, journalists ought to be using classic united front tactics against the Chinese government. They should stand together and find a way to do that. If news organizations can't do that, and I know that is difficult, press freedom organizations might be able to do it.

It is worth remembering that we have leverage with the Chinese government that we don't fully understand. The Chinese government spends millions of dollars hiring PR firms and funding their Confucius Institutes. They have a lot of things that they want from the world community including recognition as a credible player on the world stage. The foreign media are one way that they wish to shape the coverage. We could tell them that they're shaping it the wrong way.

Mae Fong (New America Foundation): There was a world media summer congress that China put together and I think this was part of their effort to project soft power. I was curious as to where it's going now because at one point it touted itself as having *New York Times* and Al-Jazeera and NBC News as its partners.

Actually it's on the brink of announcing its first ever world media summit awards, I think, in November, which is China's version of the Pulitzers. I'm curious as to where *The New York Times* is in that. My understanding is they pulled out?

70

Kahn: Xinhua, as everybody knows, is a big state news organization. It made a variety of attempts to bring together the business-side leaders of major news organizations like the leading wire services and newspapers of various countries. There were two or three of those summits, and a couple of them were attended by our publisher, Arthur Sulzberger Jr. Xinhua wanted to institutionalize them and establish that China's leading media is a peer of the leading media of the outside world. There was some willingness to go along with that as a form for dialogue between media companies. It began before the troubles that we started having in the fall of 2012. Xinhua is a fairly influential player in the state bureaucracy. The top Xinhua executive is an important Party official and offered to be helpful in trying to resolve those issues. So we didn't really have a strong incentive to make a principled point of pulling out of the Xinhua summit just for the sake of saying, "We don't have any dialogue with the Chinese."

But there had been this rotation in who hosted the meetings. I think it was decided some years in advance. Itar-Tass was supposed to host it in Moscow. They did and some point Arthur Sulzberger said, "Okay. I'll do that (in New York)."

But when it became such a contentious situation (between the *Times* and the Chinese government), I think it became clear that it wasn't viable for us to host it.

I think there should be some dialogue. Xinhua is among the most elite of the state agencies and they very much want to be a bigger part of global media. They're sending many hundreds of correspondents around the world. They want to be respected. They're evolving to some extent. They are trying to cover events, not just propagate what China is doing. They're trying to become an actual global media. Whether they will succeed in that, I have no idea. But I don't think it's fundamentally antithetical to the interests of the world media to try to see Xinhua become more international.

Jerome Cohen: Two quick questions. One for Minky—could you characterize the U.K. reaction to the Chinese failure to abide by the joint declaration? And for Joe, the interesting question is not that the visas were made so difficult, but why in the end did they allow David Barboza to stay. Was there a rationale for who gets a visa and who doesn't?

Worden: Britain co-signed the joint declaration with China. The treaty promises one country, two systems and it promises that Hong Kong people will be ruling Hong Kong with a high degree of autonomy and that this arrangement shall continue for 50 years. Britain has the principle responsibility to defend press freedom, the rule of law and the terms of the joint declaration, which are important also because they cover the rule of law. But it would have been actually better if the UK government had stayed silent. Everything that they've said has been, for want of a better word, nonsense.

The British government, for example, applauded the Chinese government's recent announcement that there would be universal suffrage in Hong Kong. As Hong Kong people understand that term, it means that you will have a choice to vote. But it doesn't mean you use your universal suffrage to vote for someone the Chinese government has pre-selected for you. British foreign policy in relation to Hong Kong and China is all about China trade. So that means that the other players like the U.S. need to step up. The time has come. They all supported the joint declaration. But if you wait for the Brits to ride to the rescue, that's going to be a very long wait.

Cohen: What about Parliament?

Worden: The Chinese government sent what can only be seen as a thuggish threat to the U.K. Parliament when they announced that they were going to investigate conditions in Hong Kong. The threat was that Britain would be harmed by such an investigation. Chris Patten, the last governor of Hong Kong, is the only person in the U.K. government who has done the right thing—and is the only person who is reminding people that John Major and Margaret Thatcher said that Hong Kong would, "never walk alone."

I don't think the U.K. Parliament is going to have enough heft to do anything. But I do think it's significant, for example, that Susan Rice (U.S. National Security Advisor) in Beijing last weekend did take up the question of the negative developments in Hong Kong. There is some hope that the U.S. and other governments can have an impact. Hong Kong is an international city. And every country has an interest in seeing that continue. Every news organization has an interest in seeing that continue because if Hong Kong is gone as a base for free reporting, China reporting is going to suffer immensely.

Cohen to Kahn: Why was David Barboza allowed to stay in China?

Kahn: I have a little understanding of why they decided not to kick David Barboza out. I don't know if I can say it is 100% certain. I guess part of it is what we heard from them and part of it is a theory. What we heard from them is that, was that *The New York Times* would be held responsible. There was a lot of hostility toward David individually. But it evolved beyond the idea that an individual correspondent was responsible for that correspondent's coverage. I think maybe they made a point of allowing David to continue to report there because the institution was being punished rather than the individual. But the second piece of it may have been that they still are reluctant to be seen as being closed to the Western press.

The expulsions that we've had are both of journalists who had in the course of a calendar year changed credentials from another organization to *The New York Times* and were then not allowed to fully process that change in credentials. So Chris Buckley was forced to leave at the end of the year after he had moved from Reuters to *The New York Times*.

He never received a credential or a visa to work for *The New York Times*. So in the bureaucratic mindset of the foreign ministry, there was no expulsion. There was merely a bureaucratic snafu.

The same happened last year with another reporter who we had hired named Austin Ramzy, who had worked for *Time* magazine. They did effectively expel people but they didn't want to acknowledge any expulsion of anybody and denied that there were expulsions.

Thomas Moore, with the Taiwan-affiliated China Institute: I want to ask about one other part of China that doesn't seem to come up at all in this conversation and that is Taiwan. Does Taiwan, either the Taiwanese press or the Taiwanese government, play any role in this?

Worden: As most people in the room know, the original one-country, two-systems model that was created by Deng Xiaoping was designed to be attractive to the compatriots in Taiwan. I think we can say that that has failed. I don't think it's such an appealing model anymore.

McLaughlin: I would say that from the data that the FCCC has collected, the journalists who often get the worst treatment when it comes to manhandling and other things like that are from Taiwan and Hong Kong and Japan. Hong Kong journalists don't have a press card. They have something else that's different. So they're in a separate category from foreign correspondents. Taiwan correspondents also have a different status. When the police are harassing journalists, they tend to look to them first.

Bill Holstein: The fact that we're sitting here and having this conversation alone represents some progress over how things have been over the last 30-some odd years. The OPC does plan to issue a statement this coming week about the outcome of this discussion and so it might be that this is useful to distribute to through various channels, this is what the OPC has to say. It might be a useful piece of leverage. My question would be, where is the FCC in Hong Kong on all this? Have they become lap dogs or do they still have a pulse? Are they still interested in these kinds of issues?

Worden: The FCC in Hong Kong has done a dynamite job of defending press freedom. They have a press freedom award and a human rights award. And also by providing a forum for many people to speak, that's another opportunity to enhance coverage. So the FCC in Hong Kong, like their cousin in China, does a terrific job.

I would also draw your attention to the Hong Kong press freedom associations. We should collaborate with them more often. And the Hong Kong Journalists Association is just a tremendous organization. They have been doing remarkable work on similar reports on conditions for journalists in Hong Kong reporting. I believe the coverage that China cares most about is the coverage in Chinese. That's why they are going after Hong Kong journalists because their coverage is often in Chinese.

Therefore the people who are truly on the front lines here are the Hong Kong journalists and the Chinese journalists. As you say, they're the ones who get manhandled, get beaten up, get threatened, get invited to tea (the Chinese euphemism for being questioned by police), the full range of unpleasant things that happen to you if you're trying to report in an unfettered way.

Susan Lawrence, Congressional Research Service: I have a question for Joe about the U.S. Congress. How helpful or unhelpful is the U.S. Congress being in these issues? The Senate passed a resolution in March supporting press freedom in China and mentioning the problems that foreign journalists are having. Did that resolution have any effect?

Kahn: Congress is a little less focused on the China question than I felt like they were back in the 1980s and '90s when senior members of Congress took a strong, largely non-partisan interest in foreign affairs. There were members on both the Republican and the Democratic side who for various reasons knew something. They traveled frequently and could shape the tone of the debate. That has now withered away a little bit.

You just don't see much diversity in the debate about China. We used to have annual most-favored nation (MFN) debates about the future of China but those don't take place anymore (because China joined the WTO). All of this is a long-winded way of saying I don't think it has had as much impact as I would hope it would have.

The administration frequently goes to China and uses the volatility and unpredictability of Congress to threaten the Chinese. It's as if they say to the Chinese, "We understand you but who knows what those crazy guys (Laughter) back in Washington are gonna do. They could really screw up the relationship." So I think Congress is useful to a certain extent in the negative sense.

Worden: Congressional support for Hong Kong has been very important. Congress has just restarted the reporting requirement under the U.S.-Hong Kong Policy Act. We have a law in

Congress that says that Hong Kong must be treated separately and that the U.S. has an interest and a stake in the preservation of freedoms in Hong Kong. The reporting has just started. There have been hearings on Hong Kong that have focused on the democracy development and press freedom. By and large, that has been useful because it's put the issues back on the administration's agenda. I do think there is still reason for hope.

Ford: Very briefly because we are the end of our session, the perception at the FCCC in Beijing is that there needs to be a more consolidated response, a joint response, or lobbying or whatever is seen as effective on this side of the Pacific to raise the profile of the issue. When Vice President Biden did bring it up, it made a difference. It's both an industry issue and press freedom issue. The onus is partly on us to do something about it. Thank you.

-0-

Subsequent commentary:

Mark Landler, writing in *The New York Times* about a summit meeting between Presidents Obama and Xi, on November 13, 2014: "The White House pushed very hard for President Xi Jinping to take questions during his news conference with President Obama at the end of their two days of meetings Wednesday...What the White House got was Xi Jingping, Unplugged, and that may have been more than it bargained for...

"Mr. Xi insisted that China protected the rights of news media organizations but that they needed to abide by the rules of the country. 'When a certain issue is raised as a problem, there must be a reason,' he said, evincing no patience for the news media's concerns about being penalized for unfavorable news coverage of Chinese leaders and their families.

"The Chinese leader reached for an unexpected metaphor to describe the predicament of *The Times* and other foreign news organizations, saying they were suffering the equivalent of a car trouble. 'When a car breaks down on the road,' he said through an interpreter, 'perhaps we need to get off the car and see where the problem lies."

PANEL 4

How Social Media and the Internet Have Transformed China Coverage

Journalists inside and outside of China are monitoring websites and social media and engaging in whack-a-mole journalism against Chinese censors.

<u>MODERATOR</u>
Susan Jakes, editor of the Asia Society's ChinaFile, who reported from Asia for *Time* and was its Beijing correspondent.

<u>PANELISTS</u>
Emily Parker, author of *"Now I Know Who My Comrades Are: Voices From the Internet Underground."*
Rose Tang, a social media activist and writer who survived the Tiananmen massacre.
David Wertime, editor of *Tea Leaf Nation* and *Foreign Policy*.

Jakes: We have the great distinction of being the panel that sits between a room full of foreign correspondents and their cocktail hour, which is a great honor. (Laughter.) I just want to introduce the panelists and then we'll get into it. I was a foreign correspondent in China at the very, very beginning of the time when nobody really used social media to do their reporting. It became an issue in the last years that I was there, 2006 and 2007. David Wertime, originally a Peace Corps volunteer in China and then a lawyer, entered journalism working purely in the field of social media. He founded a really excellent online media outlet called Tea Leaf Nation that reported on China exclusively through the use of the social media platform known as Weibo, which is a sort of Twitter-like platform. He subsequently sold

Tea Leaf Nation to what was then The Washington Post Company. His publication is now a part of *Foreign Policy* magazine and he's an editor there.

To his right, Rose Tang comes at this from a quite different angle. She was an activist in the pro-democracy demonstrations in Tiananmen Square in the late 1980s. She then worked as a journalist in traditional media for many years. More recently, she has developed a career as a generator, broadcaster, networker of dissenting opinions about Chinese politics largely on Twitter. She's working to connect disparate groups who have critiques of the Chinese regime from different angles.

And Emily Parker has the very rare distinction of having written editorials both for *The New York Times* and for *The Wall Street Journal.* She did a lot of excellent cultural coverage of China, for many years based on Hong Kong. For the past five or six years, she has really immersed herself in the study of how Chinese people were using the Internet and that research has culminated with the publication of her really excellent book on the subject earlier this year, which is called *Now I Know Who My Comrades Are: Voices From The Internet Underground.* She's now a fellow at The New America Foundation.

I thought it would be useful to ask David, who was a lawyer before he was a journalist and can speak very concisely, to give us a very brief primer on kind of the lay of the land of Chinese social media.

Wertime: Chinese social media, broadly speaking, comprises two major platforms. One is called Weibo. It has just shy of 300 million active users. The other is called Weixin and also has just around 300 million active users at last count. Weibo is like Twitter in that it is a way for one person to broadcast their views to many. So you write a short message and anybody can read it.

Weixin is, broadly speaking, a series of small groups. Friends chat with one another. Weixin also provides a platform for individuals or organizations to broadcast news to a large group of subscribers. This is called self media. Weibo was a very, very rich and vibrant space. That's changed a bit. Weixin, which is of more recent vintage, has become more popular lately, partly at the expense of Weibo. That's the short intro.

Jakes: David, continue and tell us what's changed in the space of social media over the past six months and how does it relate to how foreign journalists are doing their reporting.

Wertime: I started in journalism purely focused on this. I was reporting out of Washington, D.C. in a new media company that I had basically invented using Weibo primarily as the major source for information. That was in December 2011. There were several major stories emerging organically from Weibo on any given day—many of which were not being reported very seriously in English-language or Western media.

I can say that my job has gotten quite a bit harder over the three years that I've been doing this. That is particularly true starting in about August of 2013 when there was a crackdown on particularly high-profile users of the Weibo platform. There were people who had five, 10, 50 million followers. These were people therefore who had the ability to broadcast to this massive group of people at any given time, often with no filter between the time that they wrote their post and the time it was published.

That began to change. A number of these big opinion leaders were arrested and over the intervening year the Chinese government has basically ripped the proverbial microphone back out of the hands of the Chinese grassroots, which had taken that microphone with quite a bit of enthusiasm. So the result has been that Weibo is much less of a rich space. You have to look much harder to find a piece of breaking news or a discussion that is extremely revealing about what's happening in China. Some of those discussions still happen but they have migrated onto Weixin, which, again is like a small dinner table discussion compared to Weibo, which is more of a public rally in its most powerful moments.

We've also seen crackdowns on Weixin. A few months ago, some major public accounts on Weixin were deleted without notice. Some of the folks who were broadcasting their views to a large group of subscribers had their accounts deleted. Even more recently you have rules that basically require anybody sharing an opinion about politics or really any opinion at all through these Weixin accounts to get a government permit. It's unclear how they'll do that.

So the net effect I think is that it's gotten a lot harder to use the Chinese Internet as a source for information, which is very disappointing. The Internet in some ways is such a promising space. It has the ability to knit together so many disparate populations across China to bring the voices of the grassroots out beyond the veil to the West and to showcase the diversity of opinion and lifestyle that is the true China, the China that I knew when I was living there. So I'll end on that extremely pessimistic note.

Jakes: So some people who have sort of abandoned social media in China have moved over to Twitter, which is blocked in China, but can still get through. That's kind of the world that Rose inhabits in her work. And I thought maybe you could just talk to us a little bit about what you've been able to do over the past few months.

Tang: Thank you. I tweet mainly in Chinese for the Chinese audience. I was encouraged by one of the biggest Internet activists who has 150,000 followers on Twitter. He said, "You've got to use Twitter." I also use WeChat, a social media thing developed by a Chinese company called Tencent. It's now the most popular Chinese Internet social network.

On Twitter, I noticed every day I was getting new followers. One reason is that I put up a YouTube link of me on Twitter talking to Cui Jian, the father of Chinese rock and roll, back in February when he was screening his first feature film at New York University here. I identified myself as a survivor, a former student protester, of the Tiananmen massacre. I asked him a question and held up my phone and recorded everything he said. Then I uploaded it on YouTube.

I got so much attention. People were asking, "Who's this Rose Tang?" *Global Times*, which is a mouthpiece of the regime, called me an "unemployed housewife in Brooklyn" (where she resides) in an attempt to discredit me. They never approached me, but I had joked on Facebook to a journalist friend that I was an unemployed housewife and that's where *Global Times* picked it up. They didn't bother to check the "about" section of my Facebook account where I am clearly identified as a writer who used to work for CNN and Princeton. I still include the article on my Twitter profile. To be attacked by *Global Times* is regarded as an honor among Chinese dissidents.

The reason the *Global Times* called me a Brooklyn housewife was that I received a great deal of attention by putting up photos on Facebook of a Beijing restaurant that had a sign, which read: "This shop serves only English and Chinese. This shop does not receive Vietnamese, Filipinos, Japanese or dogs." It went viral in Vietnam, South Korea and Japan. It was covered by major news organizations. *Global Times* obviously didn't like that.

But coming back to Cui Jian. People realized that it was the first time in 25 years that he had commented on the Tiananmen Square massacre. I noticed a lot of other people online starting to talk about June 4. There were a lot of young people asking, "What are you talking about? What's June 4th?" (The government has banned any discussion of events in Tiananmen so Chinese born since 1989 have never heard about the massacre of demonstrators.) I saw hope for China because so many young people, some of them teenagers, were asking questions. They're all eager to know what's going on.

Jakes: You had a Weibo account too?

Tang: I don't use Weibo because it's useless. Because of what I advocate, I am pretty sure I would be shut down. (Laughter.) I use WeChat. I can see people inside China WeChatting as they stake out a police station where prisoners are being held. They're broadcasting it from the site. And they have group chats and they contain very outrageous comments. And especially the photos and videos. So I'm literally in touch with them at the grassroots level with a very clear agenda. The clear agenda is to overthrow the Chinese Communist Party. We're not shy about it. I put myself out there and say, "Hey, we student protesters went on a hunger strike. We went rallying and marching in 1989. And this is what the Party did. They answered our calls for a dialogue with a massacre."

So people, 25 years later, you've got to wake up. I'm calling out to the Tibetans and the Uighurs and the Mongols saying, "We've got to unite. Through our united front, we've got to overthrow the Communist Party." People inside China are talking about it and they're not shy about it.

Jakes: Presumably this is a cause that you have espoused for some time and have been working on for some time?

Tang: No, only for the past few months. I never thought it would be like this. I was encouraged by those young people inside China. Yesterday, I helped a Tibetan organization, the Tibetan

National Congress, call out to people to sign a petition to 13 Nobel peace laureates urging them to boycott a peace summit in South Africa because South African government rejected the Dalai Lama's visa under pressure from Beijing. It was the third time within five years.

So the Tibetan organization put these posts on Twitter and I translated them into Chinese. And guess what? I could not believe it. Yesterday morning there were Chinese people saying, "I want to sign it." We are talking about college students, scholars, dissidents, of course, and petitioners.

I said, "I need your location. I can help you fill out the form and I need your location, your email address, your real name." People even put their cell phone numbers down on Twitter, saying, "I'm so and so. I'm in Beijing. Or I'm in Shaanxi. And here is my cell phone number. Here is my email address. I'm signing it." This is amazing. This is the first time I've ever seen Chinese people coming out publicly supporting the Dalai Lama. And they know how dangerous it is.

Jakes: This is an extremely large change in terms of the ability of somebody living overseas to be in that kind of real-time contact with ordinary Chinese people and prominent dissidents, somebody like Hu Jia, who are under surveillance. It's kind of inconceivable that that kind of conversation could be happening.

Tang: And they're virtually open on Twitter. People are fearless. He was physically attacked really badly.

Jakes: We're going to shift the topic slightly. Another thing that social media has facilitated is more interaction between foreign journalists and their readers. Not only in terms of social media facilitating the ability of Chinese audiences to read things that the foreign press writes, but also to the point that sometimes journalists become part of the story. It seems to happen from time to time. Emily has kind of a great story to tell about that. That's the Zhu Ling case.

Parker: The Zhu Ling case, for people who are not familiar with this, this was a very strange poisoning case in the 1990s. A university student was poisoned and it was very mysterious. Nobody ever really knew what happened or who poisoned her or why. She survived but she's basically been incapacitated for life. What's really interesting in the past couple of years this story was blowing up on Weibo again. There are a lot of people on the Chinese Internet who just feel that justice was not delivered.

That's a very good way to get a lot of excitement on Chinese social media, to bring up a case where some injustice has been served. A lot of people in China believe that the poisoner had some sort of official position.

So I was on Weibo. I was just looking around. And I saw that this case was blowing up again because there had been another poisoning case at Fudan University that was totally unrelated, but it just brought back memories.

I thought, "Oh, this is interesting." I'd already done a lot of research on it. So I asked my editor at *The New Republic*, "Are you interested in a piece about this bizarre Chinese poisoning case?" And he was like, "I guess. Sure. Why not? That seems weird and interesting."

I wrote it in a very straightforward way. I said, "This is what happened in the 1990s. This is why Chinese Internet users are still so angry about this. Here's a few comments from Weibo."

When it came out in the U.S., people thought, "Oh, that's a weird, quirky story." But one of my Chinese friends put it on Weibo. He has a lot of followers. Within a matter of days, somebody, just a random Weibo user, translated it into Chinese and posted it with a link. I watched this piece rise to No. 1 on Weibo, meaning it was the piece with the most hits. Weibo has hundreds of millions of users. And it was re-tweeted or re-Weiboed hundreds of thousands of times.

So that was my first experience of actually having real Chinese readers. There is another interesting aspect to that story. When the Zhu Ling case started blowing up on Weibo at first, the censors reacted in a predictable manner by censoring it. You could no longer write her name.

Then Chinese Internet users did what they usually do, which is they misspelled her name (to evade censors). But there was so much interest in this case and there was so much energy about the case that I actually saw the censors reverse their decision. It's an interesting example of how sometimes there's just so much anger that it's not worth censoring it because it's just going to make the situation worse.

Wertime: I have never been No. 1 on Weibo, so congrats. (Laughter.) That's pretty cool. It's sort of like the experience of peering through the looking glass (a reference to Alice in Wonderland) where you pull a piece of information from Chinese media, report about it, and it somehow ends up back in Chinese media and you see the reaction to the reporting. It's fascinating to watch information ping back and forth.

This is really the frustration of dealing with the intersection between Chinese and Western media spheres. Orville Schell made a great analogy a few weeks ago, which was that these two massive spheres come into contact only at this point. That's where human beings—and it's a rather small group of human beings—find these stories and write them up and they end up on Weibo. That process doesn't occur naturally. Partly because of the existence of the Great Firewall, partly because of these sort of native platforms and partly because of language and culture, you don't have those moments as often as you would probably think.

Parker: That's totally true. I just quickly want to tell a story about it working in the opposite direction—when Chinese voices came here. It was during the whole Chen Guangcheng debacle. He was the blind activist who escaped to the U.S. embassy in Beijing. It looked like the situation was never going to end well. How was China going get out of the situation without losing face? How was the U.S. going to get out of it without looking like they were abandoning an activist?

All of a sudden it seemed like there was this happy resolution. Chen was going to just stay in China. He wasn't going to leave. And there was a line of coverage that, "Oh, China and the U.S. reached this great resolution." Chen said he wanted to kiss Secretary Clinton and everyone was so happy. There were pictures of U.S. officials, like, embracing him and holding his hand. And so everyone's celebrating this wonderful thing.

Then I remember just watching Twitter and seeing tweets coming from China. Some of the first ones were actually in English. And they were in all caps. And they said, "Chen Guangcheng talked to me. What the media reported is wrong." These were Chen's friends. They were lawyers and other activists.

The friends were using Twitter not Weibo because Chen Guangcheng is totally censored on Weibo. You couldn't say those words. The friends knew the foreign journalists were on Twitter. They wanted to talk to the foreign media. They said he was actually coerced and was pushed out of the embassy. And of course some of this turned out to be not terribly accurate either.

But the result of that was that a small group of Twitter users in China actually reversed the news cycle. In the course of a few hours, the entire narrative was different. The U.S. was suddenly on the defensive. Everyone was investigating this. So that's just one small example. I agree it's an outlier. It doesn't happen all the time, but you do see these moments where you do penetrate the other sphere.

Bill Holstein: When we first started hearing about the Internet in China, the expectation was that the Internet would change the structure of power. Many people have looked at the Internet and social media as tools by which Chinese people are going to assume a certain measure of power against the government and its censors. But we know that on the other side, government has millions of people working to control the Internet. So where are we in this battle for freedom of information? Who is winning?

Wertime: The central government has been pretty earnestly trying to bring the Internet to heel. The first serious effort that I was aware of, surely not the first was a drive for real-name registration on Weibo. The reason was a lot of people had anonymous handles or fanciful handles instead of their real names. The government felt that by requiring everyone to register with their real name, that would have a chilling effect and would make people accountable for what the government believes are rumors or negative information.

That didn't really work, for a variety of reasons. But I think, in particular, the late 2013 crackdown on Big Vs, which, again, is the colloquial term for opinion-makers with big followings on Weibo. (Big V's refers to the lead bird in a flock of geese, for example, that fly in a V formation, following their leader.) They were sort of the anchor tenants. They were the tent poles, and they brought everyone else in to sort of see what they were saying. When they lost the ability or the nerve to drive the conversation, that's had a big effect. I don't look at it as the Chinese government winning. I look at it as the Chinese government making a tactical decision that may not actually be in its long-term interest.

Clearly, they feel differently. They are certainly skilled at controlling the Internet. It's not that they censor absolutely everything, but they have a pretty developed sense of just how far they need to go to allow the Internet to develop commercially and give people the chance to blow off steam, but not threaten what they believe is their legitimacy.

The other thing I'd just add is that the Internet, on its own, is not a thing. The Internet won't do anything by itself. It's just people. That's both good and bad, right? People can be coerced. People can be bought off. But at the same time, it also shows us that just because there's been a crackdown on one platform, say Weibo, or just because one website has been shut down, or one person has been required to cancel their account on some platform, that person and their desires and their motivations aren't going away.

So you still have a great deal of latent power on the Chinese Internet. If people had complaints before the crackdown, they still have them, but they're just not voicing them. I think the government is aware that there can be massive spikes in discussion. That's really when censors crack down, when they worry that there's a destabilizing spike, when suddenly everybody's talking about something.

We saw this with what happened with attack on the Kunming train station. Suddenly, everybody was talking about this on Weibo, and there were massive discussion threads. I won't render a verdict to your question, but only time will tell. But in the last couple years, the balance has definitely shifted.

Parker: I totally agree with that assessment. From the beginning, this has been a cat-and-mouse game. The censors have always been one step behind. To a large degree, the degree of censorship in China now is just commensurate with the power of social media. As it becomes more of a potent force, yes, the censorship is amped up. So they're moving together. But the one thing that I focused on in my reporting is less the power of the Internet to spread freedom of information, but the power of the Internet to promote freedom of assembly. Or freedom of virtual assembly, at least. That is something that is far more threatening and a far greater concern to the Chinese government. Even though virtual assembly doesn't always lead to actual assembly, the Internet is an unprecedented platform for people in China to find other people who think like them and at least lay the groundwork for collective action.

Jakes: You know, I'm aware of the fact that we're sitting in a room with people who reported on the Chinese Civil War, who cabled their stories out from a cable office. The whole process of how you report has changed tremendously over the period of time represented by the people in this room. I'm just curious on behalf of my colleagues who were reporting at the same time as I was in the early 2000s in China. How much has the advent of Chinese social media changed the way that you report? Do you still go out and speak to people? Do you call people? Or do you just quote their Weibo tweets? Do you use local government Weibo accounts to do your reporting now?

Gady Epstein of *The Economist*: For me, I use all available channels. I don't quote very much from Weibo, though people like David have done a great job of that. And sometimes, local government or police department puts things out on Weibo that you wouldn't have gotten before.

Seymour Topping, formerly of *The New York Times*: As far as the civil war is concerned, you know, there's a great variance. I was in the Communist areas, covering the war, and at times, there was a certain degree of censorship at cable offices. You could generally get your copy through. On the Communist side, for instance, John Roderick of the Associated Press was able to file on the radio from Yenan, Mao's headquarters, and it was picked up by the AP.

But to get back to the modern era, my wife and I have done quite a lot of traveling to Chinese universities. On our last trip three years ago, we found we could talk freely at the universities. The Chinese government has made a decision that at the universities, it will allow a greater degree of information to encourage technological innovation. Of course, after I give a lecture at one of these universities, inevitably a professor will get up and say, "Isn't that interesting? But Mr. Topping is from a different culture where they have freedom of the press. We Chinese have another culture, another history, another set of problems, and therefore, we have to have a certain degree of censorship."

But you find at the universities, an astonishing amount of freedom. The students are much interested in a change of government to a more democratic government. Like all students, they're interested in jobs when they get out of school. But the thing that that they resent most is censorship. That's what No. 1 complaint is against the government.

They have a feeling that they have the right to know. And they use all techniques and devices to do that. I find them quite well-informed about what's going on in the world. I'm rather optimistic about the degree to which, one way or another, the Chinese people are going to have greater access to information.

Rose Tang: I agree. Imagine that, when the Tiananmen movement happened, if people had owned cell phones. Everything would have been different. That's what Chinese leaders fear the most. Emily talked about the online protests. We see a lot more online protests now. They look symbolic, but they can be very effective. And people are getting smarter and smarter and using more images in very creative ways. And images can't be censored. A few days ago, it was mid-autumn Moon Festival, which is a time for the Chinese families to have reunions. So we saw a number of wives of political prisoners online holding paper fans with a slogan. "Release so-and-so," usually their husbands' names. On the paper fans were written the Chinese characters "shandian," which means "incite and overthrow." Incite the people and overthrow the government, which is of course a crime.

One of the women was the wife of the No. 1 Mongolian dissident, who's still in jail. His name is Hada (Mongolians use only one name.) Hada's wife's name is Xinna. She was really active on Facebook. And I approached her because the information coming out of Inner Mongolia has been very sketchy. I have been working with her, translating. That's what a lot of us do, translating and editing, putting the stuff out in English instantly. It's very time-consuming and labor-intensive. But it's very effective. That's how we affect English-language media.

The reason I wanted to mention the online protest with the fans is they asked us in social media to post their pictures. "Please, put them out," they said. "Share them everywhere, on Facebook and Twitter. And send them to foreign correspondents and journalists." During the Tiananmen massacre coverage, I also was approached by correspondents in Beijing for the biggest Western news organizations and by Hong Kong journalists.

They said, "My organization wouldn't put my video, when I was doing a story for the website, but I shot this video of this Chinese dissident—who's already in jail now. Could you put it out? Could you share this?" I was overwhelmed. I said, "Oh, okay, later."

They said, "No. Share it now." I was approached by Hong Kong journalists, and saying, "We interviewed the PLA soldiers, who apologized and confessed, but we could not put so much stuff out there. Could you do it? Could you share it?"

During what's been happening in Hong Kong over the last few weeks, we've again been approached by journalists in Hong Kong, saying, "Could you share this?" So this is the funny thing. Journalists come to us now in social media. We're no longer a poor cousin to the traditional media.

Wertime to Seymour Topping: One other really interesting thing you brought up in your comment is the personalization of the experience of censorship. Tens of millions of Chinese have now actually come face-to-face with that censorship machinery— even if it's just having one post disappear. It's hard to say what the long-term impact of that will be. Is the Chinese government's current strategy going to be successful? It's still to be determined partly because of these kinds of dynamics. There's a whole generation of Chinese now who have experienced censorship personally. That erodes the credibility of government-sponsored media.

Topping: I think it is going to be very hard to continue to exercise effective censorship because of things like cloud computing. Computing is becoming much more ubiquitous because of what companies like Microsoft are doing.

Question from audience: So you have got some face-to-face with a censor. Is there any visibility into the army of censors? What do we know about those people?

Jakes: In some cases, you can actually meet them. My favorite story of a censor was the doctor who was the whistleblower about SARS in 2003. His grandson became a censor at one of the major Internet portals, and part of his job every day was to delete every mention of his grandfather's name that he came across. (Laughter.) As a user, the game is getting more and more subtle. There is increasing sophistication in the way that censorship happens.

HIGHLIGHTS & CONCLUSIONS

Ten Important Points Made During the China Hands Reunion

1. The American business community, which has enthusiastically supported U.S.-Chinese diplomatic relations, is undergoing a swing in opinion about the Chinese market and Chinese intentions. Business leaders are concerned that the Chinese government is turning up the pressure on them, through tough enforcement of anti-monopoly laws, for example, while attempting to nurture home-grown national champions that will challenge the Western incumbents. The diplomatic consequences of this shift in business opinion remain unclear.

2. Even though Chinese state-owned enterprises have not yet learned how to innovate technologically in the same way that Japanese, Korean, American and European companies have, it would be premature to count them out of the global race to the top. Flush with cash, these enterprises are acquiring technology and management experience by buying distressed assets in the West and by continuing efforts to obtain Western technology through illicit means. One way or another, the safest assumption would be that the Chinese will be competing with America's value-added industries such as semiconductors, autos and aerospace.

3. The American media has often discounted China's economic ambitions because the country insists on using a state-owned enterprise model, which most journalists see as archaic. But the Chinese are showing that their model can be made to perform at a high level.

4. The assumption that the rise of an urbanized middle class would create irresistible demands for political power is not proving to be well-founded. Increasingly affluent Chinese appear willing to accept the Communist Party's grip on power as long as it delivers economic gains to them.

5. Hopes that the Party would allow a certain measure of pluralism to be introduced as part of a "civil society" appear to be foundering. The government has engaged in a broad crackdown on dissidents and their attorneys, sought to strip local courts of decision-making authority, increased its censorship and other forms of pressure on the country's social media, sought to discipline and purify the Party to allow it to maintain its political legitimacy, and drawn a firm line against Western news organizations that engage in journalism the regime does not like. Chinese authorities at one point asked *The New York Times* to sign a statement that it would not publish objectionable news, which it refused to do.

6. The reforms that Xi is undertaking appear intended to create a smarter form of authoritarianism, rather than to embrace Western models of pluralism. His anti-corruption campaign, for example, seems reminiscent of political purges carried out under Mao Tse-tung.

7. China is rapidly going international in terms of trade, investment, education and tourism, but those trends have not led to the importation into China of Western democratic ideals and may never do so.

8. The American media does not bear the full responsibility for understanding China's economic emergence and its implications for the United States because academic and policy experts also play decisive roles. But the media's coverage has at times

appeared confused. Over the 35 years since China's normalization of relations with the United States, there have been wide swings in the tone of coverage.

9. It has been extremely difficult for correspondents to find exactly the right balance in their coverage of China because, as participants noted, it is a country where opposite trends often seem to be occurring at the same time. Editors back home are not interested in highly nuanced stories. They want "good" or "bad" stories, not ones that are too complex.

10. Chinese use of social media has exploded but the government's censors have maintained their ability to watch for sudden spikes in activity and defuse them. The government wants the Internet to be a tool for technological innovation and economic growth, but is determined to prevent it from undermining its political control.

APPENDICES

APPENDIX A: List of Attendees*

Last	First	Background
Alexander	Jan	China/Hong Kong for Newsweek International, now Institutional Investor/Alpha
Band	Allan	WSJ.com ExpatLife Columnist
Bao	Beibei	OPC Foundation winner
Barreda	David	ChinaFile: photo/visuals editor
Becquelin	Nicolas	Senior Researcher, Asia Division, Human Rights Watch
Bell	Matthew	ChinaFile photo/visuals editor
Bogert	Caroll	Human Rights Watch, former Newsweek
Brauchli	Marcus	Correspondent in China, then managing editor, Wall Street Journal, Washington Post
Brooks	Adam	Former BBC Beijing; author of *Night Heron*, espionage thriller in China
Bussey	John	Previously based in Hong Kong and Tokyo, now Wall Street Journal assistant managing editor
Chen	Kathy	Former Wall Street Journal in China
Chen	Liyan	Guest of John Koppisch/Forbes reporter
Cohen	Jerome	New York University law professor, longtime China specialist
Crovitz	Gordon	Former editor, Far Eastern Economic Review, now Wall Street Journal columnist
Demick	Barbara	LA Times-outgoing Beijing bureau chief; current fellow at Council on Foreign Relations
Dunleavy	Yvonne	Hong Kong-based Australian journalist, now OPC member in New York
Elliott	Dorinda	Paulson Institute; Previously worked in Asia for Newsweek, BusinessWeek, Asiaweek
Engardio	Pete	Boston Consulting Group; Business Week, Hong Kong; author
Epstein	Gady	Economist Beijing Bureau Chief
Ferguson	Tim	Forbes Asia editor, OPC Treasurer
Fingleton	Eamonn	Euromoney Asia Editor in 1980s; Author
FlorCruz	Jaime	40 years in Beijing, CNN
Fong	Mei	New America Foundation; former WSJ Hong Kong & China 2003-09
Ford	Jocelyn	Based in Beijing, representing Foreign Correspondents Club of China

Frank	Allan Dodds	OPC board member
Fry	Sonya	Retired OPC Executive Director
Glimcher	Sumner	OPC member
Goldstein	Richard	Guest of Roy Rowan
Holstein	William	UPI/ Hong Kong and Beijing, 1979-1982; former OPC president
Ignatius	Adi	Harvard Business Review; Time Asia/Wall Street Journal
Jakes	Susan	Editor of Asia Society's ChinaFile; Time Beijing correspondent
Kahn	Joseph	Based in China for the New York Times, now NYT foreign editor
Kazer	William	Wall Street Journal, Beijing
Klein-Ahlbrandt	Stephanie	Just moved to New York from China; FCCC member
Koppisch	John	Forbes, senior editor for Asia; Asian WSJ 1995-2000
Kranz	Patricia	OPC Executive Director
Landreth	Jonathan	ChinaFile managing editor, who reported from Beijing 2004-2012
Lawrence	Dune	Bloomberg Beijing 2006-9
Lawrence	Susan	Congressional Research Service; worked in Beijing for Wall Street Journal, U.S. News, Far Eastern Economic Review
Lee	Abby	Taipei Economic and Cultural Office
Lubman	Sarah	Once based in China, now PR with Brunswick Group, OPC Board Member
Mabry	Marcus	OPC president/New York Times
Mahoney	Robert	Committee to Protect Journalists Deputy Director
McLaughlin	Kate	Global Post, Bloomberg BNA/China 2002-2014
Meng	Meng	Bloomberg, OPC Foundation winner
Moore	Thomas	China Institute vice president
Morrison	Timothy	CNN, Asiaweek, Time 1997-2008
Mott	Glenn	Hearst Syndicate, Managing editor; Beijing, Hong Kong
Mrevlje	Andrej	Guest of Elizabeth Rosenthal
Nagorski	Andrew	Former Newsweek, now at East-West Center
Olesen	Alexa	Tea Leaf Nation writer; covered China for AP
Osnos	Evan	New Yorker, China, recent author of *The Age of Ambition*
Osnos	Sarabeth	Guest of Evan Osnos
Parker	Emily	Author, *Now I Know Who My Comrades Are. . .*
Pesta	Abigail	Covered Hong Kong for Forbes 1992-94; OPC vice president

Ping	An	Forbes, Hong Kong, now Committee of 100
Rosenthal	Elizabeth	New York Times, Beijing 1997-2003
Rowan	Roy	Life, Fortune; Covered Chinese civil war
Schell	Orville	Covered China for the New Yorker, Atlantic, etc., now Asia Society
Schiereck	Joost	Guest of Yvonne Dunleavy
Tang	Rose	Social media activist and Tiananmen survivor
Topping	Seymour	Retired AP, New York Times, covered the Chinese civil war
Topping	Audrey	Photojournalist/author/filmmaker specializing in Chinese affairs
Tyson	James	Christian Science Monitor Beijing; author *China Awakenings*
Weatherman	Bess	Warburg, Pincus
Wertime	David	Editor of *Tea Leaf Nation* and *Foreign Policy*
Worden	Minky	Based in Hong Kong for many years, now with Human Rights Watch
Yang	Yifan	SIPA student, NYT researcher in Beijing
Zhang	Yuwei	China Daily New York
Zimmerman	Jamie	Litespeed Partners

*List is approximate. A handful of those who accepted invitations to come may not have actually attended, while others who did not RSVP did appear.

APPENDIX B: FCC Policy Paper Summary

A summary of the policy paper by the Foreign Correspondents Club of China regarding the government's increasingly heavy-handed techniques used against Western correspondents and their organizations:

China's ruling Communist Party continues to erect hurdles to foreign journalists, and the media companies that employ them, discouraging reporting on many aspects of China. Foreign journalists are restricted in where they can travel. Their sources are vulnerable to intimidation or worse. If they or their co-workers write stories that displease the Chinese government, they face retribution. This could come in the form of threats, effective expulsion (visas not being renewed), retribution against news assistants and reprisals against a journalist's media company that has business interests in China.

In a Foreign Correspondents' Club of China (FCCC) survey this year of China-based foreign correspondents, 80% of those surveyed thought that their work conditions had worsened or stayed the same compared to 2013. The FCCC believes that China is rapidly eroding the progress it made in "opening up" to the world prior to the 2008 Olympics. In the years since the 2008 Beijing Olympics, there has been a notable increase in threats and use of violence against foreign journalists, their staff, and their sources; China's restrictive and punitive visa practices have severely hampered global news organizations' coverage of China. In 2014, China is further away from making good on its pre-Olympic pledges to uphold a "policy of opening up to the outside world" and to protect the lawful rights of foreign journalists.

China's poor record on allowing open and unfettered reporting is in conflict with its desire to be seen as a modern society deserving of global respect. And it is in great contrast with the wide access Chinese journalists have enjoyed when reporting in many foreign countries.

As China embraces and leverages press freedoms abroad for its own media, it is going the opposite direction at home. Authorities maintain strict control and censorship over domestic journalists. China's policies toward and treatment of the international media have not matched the nation's advances toward international norms in other areas.

The FCCC advocates a free reporting environment for all. Foreign reporters in China should enjoy the same access and freedoms that Chinese reporters enjoy in most other countries. Media organizations should enjoy the same freedom to disseminate their work in China that Chinese media organizations enjoy in most other countries. The FCCC advocates the elimination of barriers to free reporting and the establishment of a level playing field. The FCCC welcomes enhanced dialogue with authorities to improve mutual understanding and work out standard operating procedures for smoother coverage of news events.

To read the full position paper please visit the FCCC website at www.fccchina.org.

APPENDIX C: OPC of America Press Release

Overseas Press Club of America Protests Growing Threats to Media Freedom in China and Hong Kong

NEW YORK, New York –Sept. 16, 2014 — For more than 75 years, Overseas Press Club members have reported news from China and Hong Kong, advancing the world's understanding of China.

But within the past year, conditions for reporting in China have deteriorated sharply with threats, intimidation, censorship, and denials of work visas. International news media and the Chinese press are under pressure not seen since 1989, the year of the Tiananmen Square demonstrations and military crackdown. That reality was underscored during a reunion of some 70 current and former China and Hong Kong correspondents held in New York on Sept. 12, and by the most recent position paper of the Foreign Correspondents Club of China.

As China plays a larger role in global politics and economics, the country has failed to maintain its commitment to free flows of information. Instead, China's growing power on the world stage has led to attacks, bullying of international news organizations, and reprisals against Chinese reporters. Chinese writers and journalists have been arrested and given harsh sentences; international reporters have been banned from covering some geographic areas; Chinese news assistants to Western correspondents have been threatened; websites with critical reporting have been blocked; and social media reporting has been suppressed.

Such roadblocks to coverage do damage to China and its 1.3 billion citizens, feeding the perception that China is not politically and economically stable and is not willing to follow international norms.

In the past, China's leaders have recognized the value of free flows of information: China's constitution protects freedom of speech and of the press. In the run-up to the 2008 Beijing Olympics, the government committed itself to allowing expanded and unfettered reporting by Western news organizations.

Similarly, for decades, Hong Kong has been an oasis of free speech and a robust media—both among local media and journalists from around the world who have been based there. This status is now at risk.

Recent alarming events in Hong Kong demand urgent focus. In 1984, China signed an international treaty, the Joint Declaration, expressly guaranteeing press freedom in Hong Kong and the continued application of the International Covenant on Civil and Political Rights. This treaty is registered at the United Nations.

The escalation of violent attacks on journalists and demands from China's Central Liaison Office for censorship and to cease advertising in independent media are causes for great concern. If Hong Kong loses its free flow of information, the territory will quickly lose its status as a global financial center.

Press freedom is most likely to advance over time in China if it is preserved today in Hong Kong.

We urge Chinese leaders to reverse course and enforce their own laws requiring free speech and press freedom. China's future progress and its engagement with the world depend on it.